Fred Dibnah
A MUCH LOVED STEEPLEJACK

Fred Dibnah

Dr. Fredrick Dibnah MBE
1938 - 2004

This book is dedicated to all Fred Dibnah fans throughout the world

Fred Dibnah
A MUCH LOVED
STEEPLEJACK

Written by
Fred Dibnah MBE
Sheila Dibnah
Paul Donoghue

Illustrations by International artist Brian Smith

Fred Dibnah
A MUCH LOVED STEEPLEJACK

Compiled and edited: **Paul Donoghue**

Design: **David Smith Opus64 Nottingham**

Project Editor: **Colleen Donoghue**

Photographs: **The Paul Donoghue Heritage Collection**

Additional contributions & photographs: **Sheila Dibnah, Neil Carney, Alf Molyneux, Peter Johnson, Stuart Radford, David Jack, Mary Maxfield, David Hall Eddy Chattwood and EMPICS**

Illustrations: **Brian Smith**

Produced for Rallyscene
The Pond House
59 Rotherham Road
Clowne
Derbyshire
S43 4PT

Website: **www.freddibnah.tv**

Email: **freddibnahtv@aol.com**

Telephone: **01246 81112**

Printed by: **William Gibbons & Son. Wolverhampton**

Copyright: **Paul Donoghue**

ISBN 1-59971-963-0

Contents

Contents

A WOMAN IN THE KNOW
Forward by Sheila Dibnah

A name like Dibnah naturally leaves it's mark. I am often asked what it was like being married to 'Our Fred,' but so far no one has asked me to write it down. Until now. I welcome the opportunity to give you, the reader a snap-shot glimpse into my world.

A lot has happened to me since Fred died, and not all good. I shall eventually deal with these issues in a separate book, and take you on that rumbling, chugging ride through the odious fog left in the aftermath of an industrious, celebrated life.

The colourful character of complexities ...

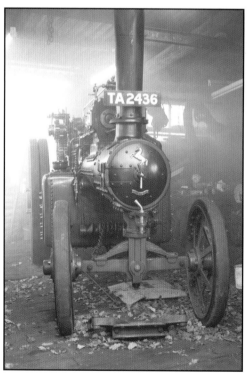

But for the time being, I hope you enjoy taking a peek into what exactly made Fred tick. The colourful character of complexities that he became not only to a public who adored him, but also to friends and family. What you saw is what you got. And this book compiled by Paul Donoghue, who came into Fred's life long before I did, gives readers some of the zeniths of the man as Steeplejack, Steam Expert, Historian and the person we knew as 'our Fred'. Several years ago, Paul spent time with Fred and his second family, and as you will see, has amassed an astonishing amount of material. By a peculiar twist of fate, I knew Paul's wife Colleen, a striking lass from Blackpool, many years ago during my time as a showgirl in the resort. We lost touch, and only became friends again much later after Fred had died and so I am delighted to be associated with this publication.

What can I say about Fred that hasn't already appeared in print? Well, I can tell you exactly what he was like to live with. How his 'obsessions' with steam, engineering, coal mining and all things mechanical shaped our lives. I can tell you about his love of a pint or two and what he expected from a traditional wife. The trouble is – so can two other Mrs Dibnahs! What they cannot know however, is how illness and sheer tenacity to get his Aveling & Porter Colonial Steam Tractor finished affected his final years. Nor can they deal with the direct effect of the increasing amounts of people in our lives towards the end...

The Tall Blonde

came into his life in 1996 and things looked up – especially Fred, who at 5'5" didn't feel the least intimidated that I towered above him at 5'10". It has been suggested that if you put a thousand people side by side and paired them up, then I wouldn't be in the last fifty! However, none of that mattered, because somehow, we grew to love each other. I think he also considered me quite mad, because I liked cast iron and had a bit of a fetish about spanners, so that helped to oil the wheels of a love affair with Mr Dibnah!

My life will never be the same again. But then, all of us feel that way – maybe that is why you have decided to buy this book? He was a good man, my husband. He rightly deserves to be remembered and, although there can only ever be one of his kind, I just hope that the following stories - most of which have never before been available before - will prompt his fans and followers to forever remember him and all that he achieved.

Sheila Dibnah

THE BOOK THAT NEVER WAS?
THE STORY OF MR. SMITH - A LANCASHIRE STEEPLEJACK
BY FRED DIBNAH

As the Victorian factory owner's empires steadily grew, and more chimneys shot up skywards, they realised nobody had given much thought on how they were going to maintain them. They couldn't just close the works, whilst somebody went up the inside and examined the chimney, because obviously, this would lose the company vast sums of money and interrupt output.

The usual method of 'laddering' a chimney is said to have been the brainchild of Mr Smith, the famous Lancashire Steeplejack. Joseph Smith was born in Coventry and was quite young when he came to live in Rochdale, Lancashire. Standing at five feet five and a half inches tall, he had a striking presence and appears to have been a man of very few words. He seems to have been rather a serious sort of chap in some ways, and unlike most steeplejacks, he didn't smoke or drink either! I think he must have been a bit of a character though, because he went about the country in a Pullman Coach, and was considered something of a gentleman, as he liked to dress in a jacket and tie.

In 1995 film producer Paul Donoghue was invited to collate a book about Fred's life. The book was to be called "Fred Dibnah The Lancashire Steeplejack". There had already been a book of the same name published in 1902 by George Falconer.

The subject of the book was a famous Steeplejack called Joseph Smith.

Fred was fascinated by the Smith book and decided to tell the story of Joseph Smith in his own words. What follows is the first chapter of a book that due to Fred's increasing fame and television commitments had to be shelved.

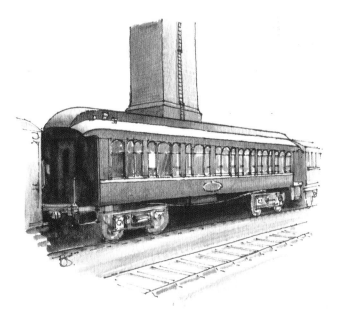

11

So, Mr Smith had his own beautiful Pullman wagon purposely built for his own use.

From what I can gather, like many men of his time, Mr Smith lived his life as a fearless, relentless individual, who undertook the task in hand with great vigour. He lived in a time when there were a great many chimney disasters, such as the collapse of the Newlands Mill chimney in Bradford on 28th December 1882. Fifty-four people were killed and many injured. This was caused by attempts to straighten the thing, by other steeplejacks.

Again, at Huddersfield on 18th November 1893, a chimney was brought down in a gale. An inexperienced steeplejack, on the advice of the mill owner, had heightened it by over thirty feet. Then another ten heightened the chimney again without any consideration that the base of the thing was only six feet square. It came tumbling down, killing two men, and caused considerable damage to the surrounding properties.

It seems he started out as a scaffolder, and slowly took up steeplejacking. To all intents and purposes, he was very successful, and would travel great distances to mend, straighten and fell chimneys. To be mending a chimney in say Coventry, and the business of steeplejacking being controlled by the weather, it was difficult to go into lodgings if for a number of days you couldn't work, and later faced with a big accommodation bill.

Also, in those days, lodgings were sometimes a bit dodgy, with damp beds, cold, dirty rooms, and rotten food. In the days before environmental health departments and the health and safety officer, to have a caravan, and live on the job in nice cosy warm conditions – a bit like the fairground men – was much better. So, Mr Smith had his own beautiful Pullman wagon purposely built for his own use. It had oriental mirrors, fine furniture and all the necessary cooking paraphernalia. This was loaded on a goods train; and was pulled to the next town he was working in. The ladders, planks, ropes and other equipment followed on in another coach.

Another disaster tells a similar tale, and this one was called 'The Great Cleckheaton Chimney Disaster'. This stack was at Marsh Mills, Cleckheaton, in Yorkshire and was undergoing repair when, on the 24th February 1892 it collapsed, killing fourteen people. They had kept on building and building this stack, and at 180ft high, it got a bit top heavy for its base of about 45 feet diameter. Circular, weighing in at about 500 tons, it crashed down for about 70ft on its haunches and leaned over and fell down on the mill, destroying it in the process.

There is a tale of him working at the top of a chimney with his assistant who suddenly went doolally.

It is easy to see why Mr Smith had such a good reputation, as there are no records of him causing any disasters or owt like that, or being incompetent in any way. This guy knew what he was doing and so was in much demand. He did have great moments of courage as well, like when he faced unexpected danger. There is a tale of him working at the top of a chimney with his assistant who suddenly went doolally.

They were up on a scaffold at Sutcliffe's Corn Mill, near the old Railway Station in Rochdale. Suddenly, this particular workman who was with him gave out an almighty wail and leapt into space. As he went over the edge, Mr Smith is reputed to have seized him by the ankle, and the crazed man hung like a dead weight, writhing and shrieking in the air. Struggling, with great effort, he pulled the man up, until he could seize his belt. Having got a firm hold of this, he then pulled him back onto the platform, where the unfortunate man started to furiously punch Mr Smith, and the two men battled it out between themselves on a narrow platform 200ft up in the air. So desperate was he to do himself in by jumping off, he tried to bite himself free, and for the rest of his life, Mr Smith was said to bear scars of this appalling, violent incident.

It wasn't quite over yet. As it became obvious desperate measures were called for; becoming weak himself, Mr Smith bopped the crazed madman a stunning blow over the head with a small iron crowbar for their joint safety. But even this was not enough, and before the star-crossed man was finally subdued, another hard blow was needed.

Mr Smith found it then possible, by tying a piece of rope attached to the man's belt, to lower him safely to the ground. By the time he reached land dangling from the rope, this peculiar fellow had almost become conscious again.

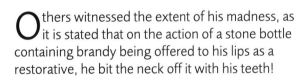

Others witnessed the extent of his madness, as it is stated that on the action of a stone bottle containing brandy being offered to his lips as a restorative, he bit the neck off it with his teeth!

The crazed man eventually recovered; the terrible incident was witnessed by a large number of people at Rochdale station who were waiting for their trains, and were totally gobsmacked by what they'd just seen.

I fancy it might all be a bit of an exaggeration, but even if it is, it is still a good tale. Mind you, it might be true, because most steeplejacks are bloody mad anyway!

Curiously, Mr Smith regarded his most perilous climb, the one where he went up Rochdale Town Hall for 265ft. This was done to place a flag on the summit on the anniversary of the birthday of a late statesman. The climb was nothing in itself, but this particular one meant shinning up a lightning conductor hand over hand to reach the top. He found the conductor very unsafe, but not being a faint-hearted sort of chap in any way, he carried on regardless of his own safety. He eventually got to the top, and there another difficulty awaited him. In those days, an antique and fearsome ornament of the figure of St. George was up there as a substitute for a weathercock. It was his task to climb up on the shoulders of this thing, and lash around its chest an 18 feet pole to attach the flag to. He managed this task, wobbling about with not much footholding to the amazement of the crowd below that shouted and cheered. It became part of local history, and at the time, people talked about it for years afterwards. "The Brave Mr Smith – the Lancashire Steeplejack."

What you have to remember though, is that blokes like him were sometimes admired as much as television personalities are today, because nothing much was happening in peoples' daily lives like now. It was a form of entertainment for the people to see a couple of blokes balancing up there, on top of a chimney, or swinging about on a bosun's chair; it was quite a remarkable sight. The Victorians had a splendid sense of drama as well, so this would be an ideal situation for anyone who was a writer at that time to display their talents to anyone fortunate enough to be able to read. But how far some of these reported tales about Mr Smith go as to being totally accurate, nobody really knows. Like one, which reports he was working at the top of a chimney that was out of plumb by a great degree, when suddenly he heard a groan and knew the chimney was about to tumble. He then slipped quickly down a lifeline and fled for his life, just as the thing crashed over to the ground within ten yards of him. I've heard tell that once, whilst removing dangerous coping stones from the top of a factory chimney, one fell off, hit the scaffolding and carried it way from beneath his feet. He managed to throw himself against the very top edge of the chimney, which was the usual nine inches thick. His head and shoulders were hanging over the inside, his legs being over the outside. Scorched and suffocated by the hot, sulphurous air and smoke, he managed to work himself round to the ladders on the other side of the chimney, enabling him to reach the ground safely.

I'll tell you in a minute about another one. Now, I do find this one very hard to accept as anything like true, because having spent my life around chimneys great and small, I can't believe he fell off one and just walked away! What is certain though; for all intents and purposes, he possessed a muscular constitution the strength of an ox, with an easy-going attitude, planning everything out carefully beforehand, and could accurately judge distances and measurements by the eye. Not such a bad way for a bloke working as a steeplejack to be. The supposed story where he fell off a chimney happened in August 1887. Having safely fixed a lightning conductor on a new steeple at Friarmere Church in Delph, he then left to fix a mill chimney at Linfitts. The chimney was about 75ft high, and as usual he had fixed the ladders one above the other, much the same as I do today. But on this occasion, whilst fixing the last section, it collapsed, and the ladder fell to the ground, with him on it.

I'll tell you in a minute about another one. Now, I do find this one very hard to accept as anything like true...

Carried into a local cottage by onlookers, they were amazed to find he was still alive. A doctor rushed to the scene shortly afterwards, and was reputedly astonished to find him not only alive, but no bones were broken. With the exception of a few bad bruises, Mr Smith was then able to walk unaided to a waiting cab on his own accord. I've got an old copy of a little book written about him in 1898, which ends this story by saying, "Mr Smith was none the worse for his tremendous fall"

Some guy, eh - bu-bum!

Not only did he undertake alteration and restoration work, but naturally he felled chimneys too. One of the first sets of pictures taken of a chimney felling were his, just outside Walsden Railway station in Lancashire.

Mr Smith had been commissioned to undertake this work by The Lancashire and Yorkshire Railway Company. The chimney was made of stone, stood at 135ft, and weighed about four hundred tons. So, it wasn't such a very big one. The greatest chimney he felled was an octagonal one at Higher Broughton, Manchester. The stack was 270 feet high, 92 feet in circumference and 7 feet 8 inches thick at the base. They reckon it contained 1,000,000 bricks and weighed about 4,000 tons.

The chimney, because of it being such a big one, took him and five of his men eight days to cut away the base, and underpin it with 130 props. One problem he faced about bringing this big bugger down was that it leaned in the opposite direction they wanted it to fall. By all accounts, he did a grand job, and was complimented on his underpinning technique by Sir Leader Williams, the engineer for the Manchester Ship Canal, who witnessed it, along with another twenty thousand spectators on the day.

A very dangerous thing to do is straightening a very tall chimney that is leaning - or out of plumb. I've done this myself, and it needs very careful planning and skilful attention for the operation to become a success. One in particular that Mr Smith attempted is mentioned in my little book I have about him and is worth repeating. A round stack measuring nearly 200ft was no less than 4 feet and 6 inches out of plumb. The method used goes like this:

The chimney, because of it being such a big one, took him and five of his men eight days to cut away the base

In order to straighten it, he cut out a course of brickwork from the convex sides with chisels. Then a series of iron wedges, varying in size from about 3 feet, to 6 inches, were temporarily substituted for the course of bricks. When this was complete, then the real tricky stuff came about.

The smaller wedges were withdrawn first, followed by the larger, the gaps being filled with a thinner course of bricks and mortar. So, as the wedges were taken out, the stack gradually returned to the perpendicular by the force of gravity, and finally it was brought back into a true plumb line. Goes without saying really, but it's a very delicate operation, and extremely dangerous. Just that little too much violence or too much brickwork removed and then - WHAM! The whole structure would become unstable and topple over. Experience shows that in most cases, a single cut would be enough to straighten a chimney, but occasionally it is necessary to make as many as four. The stack I mention here that Mr Smith worked on needed three such cuts before it was straight again.

However, without a doubt, the thing he is most likely to be remembered for are his laddering techniques still in use today. 'The Lancashire Way' is a bit different from how Yorkshire steeplejacks would ladder a chimney, as their ladders stand away from the chimney wall, and it is the way I have always done my chimneys. Good bloke that Mr Smith ... I would have liked to have met him along with Joseph Ball of Oldham, a steeplejack from Oldham, who was a bit mad too.

'The Lancashire Way' is a bit different from how Yorkshire steeplejacks would ladder a chimney

He was a charismatic, eccentric man, who started out as a chimney sweep, later becoming a steeplejack. He had ideas of grandeur, and eventually went on to build his own castle in the middle of a row of terraced houses!

By all accounts, he had a charming, persuasive manner and despite being very intelligent, was totally illiterate, and never got beyond signing his own name. Not only that, he would at times speak in a nonsensical way, by misusing and jumbling words around, punctuating his sentences by throwing in big words, similes and resorting to sarcasm when the need arose. In spite of these odd quirks and liberties he took with the Queen's English, it was easy to gather his meaning, and he became very successful in business.

Certainly a character, he always wore a tightly fitting black suit - the trousers exceedingly short and almost too tight - large, coffin-like boots, a white shirt front with a two and a half inch stand up collar, worn without a tie, and a black bowler hat. Perhaps from his description, Laurel and Hardy managed to get some inspiration from him! That would have pleased him no end, because he moved in theatrical circles, as well as being a steeplejack.

As a young boy, working as a chimney sweep, his paradise on earth was the glittering lure of the Musical Halls. His mind was captivated by painted ladies of dubious repute, swinging their limbs about for all to see. This would prevail for all his life, and was to influence him later. But his canny business mind, sense of the theatrical and almost naturally instinctive way he had of relating to people, brought him a fair bit of reward in the steeplejacking job.

Once, for instance, when he had to visit Lord Salisbury at Hadfield House on a business matter, it was typical of him to seize the moment. As they stood at the front of the mansion, suddenly Mr Ball scrambled up the downspout to prove a point, frightening the poor Marquis to death almost. No doubt, he got the job!

These men were my steeplejacking heroes as a kid, and I once went to see where Joe Ball is buried in Oldham Cemetery. Funny that – I would have thought the poor bugger would have died with his boots on at the top of some chimney, but he didn't!

Ah well...

LIFE OF A STEEPLEJACK

BY

FRED DIBNAH

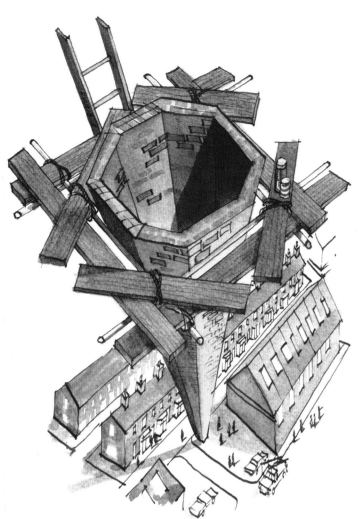

Imagine it. You're stuck on the top of a two-hundred-and-odd-foot factory chimney. It is winter, frosty, blowing a gale, and starting to rain; you can feel the damned thing swaying in the wind. It's taken a fair bit of effort to get up here in this filthy weather, but somehow, you manage to concentrate on the task of doing repairs and mending the thing until it's time to go down for a butty and a couple of pints at dinner time.

All my life I've known what sheer hard effort this game is. Yet, I enjoy it. Especially on a nice warm sunny day, swinging about on my bosun's chair, with a paintbrush; or doing a bit of pointing with my trowel. Up here, you are your own boss. You can ponder on what you have to do next on your steam engine back home, and watch life go peacefully by. Yeah, I loved days like that. Definitely!

A lot of folk don't seem to appreciate that in the past, there were dozens and dozens of blokes doing this same job, week in - year out. Some steeplejacks worked as a one-man-band and others set up businesses between themselves, employing many 'operatives' (as they refer to them today). Most worked on their own patch, and there was never a shortage of work for these men. It was a good living in some respects, and had an element of dark, dangerous glamour about it.

From about 1700 to 1800, industrial chimneys were usually square and not very tall, perhaps no more than about 30ft high, and were built as part of the engine house. Then along came along Mr. James Watt, with his first steam engines in 1776. The boilers for these needed much stronger draught, so larger freestanding chimneys had to be built to create this effect; and instead, were connected to the boiler by flues.

With taller chimneys, the base had to be much thicker to deal with the increased weight of stone or brickwork. It wasn't necessary to take this up the full height of the stack, so they had a characteristic tapering appearance called 'the batter' as the walls got thinner and thinner towards the top.

But it wasn't until the first part of the nineteenth century, and the grand mechanisation of the cotton industry with steam power, that wealthy industrialists needed to build even bigger, better and taller chimneys. These gradually became more ornate, sporting fancy tops and brickwork all cleverly designed, so they reflected the owners' money and status in society, as well as being functional.

The mill chimney, by nature of the way it worked, had to be designed by specialists in the field, and such men were called 'factory engineers' in Lancashire. The many aspects of chimney building needed a good educated man with a brain to be able to calculate wind pressures in relation to the height, weight, diameter and the form of construction. They used graphics to work this out, and would consider the materials to be used in connection with the nature of the industry that the firm was involved in producing, as well. Also, a lot of guesswork was done, as they all came to different conclusions, and couldn't reach an agreement about it.

Once a design had been agreed upon, specialist chimney builders then undertook the construction. Considering the amount of work involved, it is pretty amazing to think in some cases, such as Blinkhorn's large chimney in Bolton, stood at no less than 369ft 6ins, and was built within sixteen weeks from the word go.

A lot of folk don't seem to appreciate that in the past, there were dozens and dozens of blokes doing this same job, week in - year out.

At the turn of the century, it was quite common to cut the first sod, build a cotton mill, and have it spinning cotton within twelve months. That meant they would build a five-storey high mill, equip it with about four Lancashire boilers, a two hundred feet chimney, and a steam engine.

However for the chimney, after the foundation had been established, if it was a circular one, which was the easiest to build, the rest of the job was fairly simple. The octagonal or square chimneys tended to be older ones built around about the 1890's and 1900's. In Lancashire cotton districts, they had a tendency to build these. It is amazing that from town to town they were different, because local chimney building specialists built them all. For instance, around Preston, there were a heck of a lot of square ones and in Bolton, they tended to be octagonal shaped. Later on, by 1910, nearly everywhere they were building round ones.

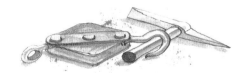

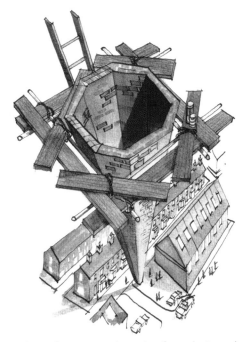

When they started on the foundation, they had a block of wood, a piece of string and a six-inch nail. If it was a circular chimney, the man held the block of wood in the middle of the foundation, and the other guy holding the string (which was roughly half the diameter of the basement course) wandered round with the nail, closely followed by the foreman bricklayer. He laid an outside course of bricks in circular form, all the way round. Then they would do the same again, with another course about four feet inside the first. Then they spread the semi-liquid mortar with a paddle like a garden hoe, in gap. They put the bricks in dry; they didn't lay them with a trowel, one bed at a time, all the way round. Then the next outside course went up, then the same thing again, but an inch stepped in. Liquid mortar again, which ran between the head joints of the brickwork underneath, and then more dry bricks. They carried on doing this, and gradually, it's coming up like a pyramid. What you ended up with is a practically solid mass – no air holes or 'owt.

So if it started of say, ten bricks thick on the bottom, twenty-odd feet up it went to nine bricks.

You could stand on it easily, but as it got gradually thinner going up, they started leaving four bricks out on the inside course, and put two putlogs across, that's two pieces of wood; and a decking made of tongue-and-groove boards, with a trap door in the middle, like in a windmill. So if anybody dropped a brick it meant the poor bloke at the bottom loading the bricks in the tub didn't get one on his head!

Large factory chimneys were always constructed like this – working up from the inside, without the use of any scaffolding, moving the wooden platform up as required. As the chimney got higher, about every six feet or so, they left out another four bricks, and put another two putlogs across and then built another platform, by moving the last one up. There are a lot of variations on this method though, basically, it is the same. Sometimes, about every thirty feet, they would leave bricks out. That means they would put the first platform up, and when they got six feet up, they would just erect four thirty-feet tall poles, lash two pieces of timber across and place another wooden deck on there. It couldn't fall over, because it was trapped inside the brickwork. Roughly every fifteen to twenty feet, the brickwork steps in half a brick. So if it started of say, ten bricks thick on the bottom, twenty-odd feet up it went to nine bricks. Then eight bricks, then seven, and then six! Right up to the top, until the wall ended up about nine inches thick.

And even though many were only this wide at the top, almost the thickness of a garden wall, some of them had stone work on, which reached out into space for about five feet! How the hell did they balance that on top of a great chimney?

It never ceases to amaze me, how they must have struggled getting them on. There is no way it could have been done easily. The other thing – the ones that were built at the turn of the century, especially in areas like Lancashire, had terracotta tops. Beautiful, bright red fancy moulded tops. These were all hollow segmental pieces, and even though they were about six feet long and two feet across, once you had them into position on the top of a chimney, they were filled in with concrete to give then strength. It created one solid lump of what looked like bright red brick.

When there were four big boilers in action at the bottom, that chimney never went cold as long as the mill was in business so they were impervious to the weather. But later, when boilers became more economical, and later still when bad times came and the mill shut down, it was terrible news for terracotta-topped chimneys, because the damp got in, and they froze, which cracked them apart. The sulphur content of the coal smashed and expanded them, which meant great lumps would come tumbling down; so most of the terracotta ones have now been destroyed.

So you see, although folk remember me for being on telly as a steeplejack and knocking chimneys down, not many wonder about those poor blokes who had to build them in the old days.

22

A Steeplejacks Dream

THEY CAME FROM THE BBC
BY FRED DIBNAH

I had in my opinion reached the peak of my career; I had got a job mending the Town Hall clock in Bolton, which is the biggest building in the town. I'd made 16 stone pillars for the balustrade around the top of the lantern, and the job was going well.

O ne day the public relations man appeared from the Bolton Council and said, "Next Thursday Look North West are coming to see you about going on the news", and I thought "God that's television", and if you've never been on tele and you're somebody like me it's a scary sort of thing.

T hursday morning came and me and Donald were up in the lantern 200 foot up in the sky. A grey van arrives on the precinct down below, with the words BBC on the side. They got out, put the tripod up and put the howitzer on, as I call it.

I thought "God that's television", and if you've never been on tele and you're somebody like me it's a scary sort of thing

25

The man whose coming to do the interview has the reputation of being a mountaineer and a rock climber, so I thought this will be a really good interview because he won't be afraid of walking on a bloody plank 200 foot in the sky will he if he's a mountaineer?

To get to where I am they have to use a lift for two storeys, then it's shanks pony up wooden staircases through the clock and the bell frame, up high ladders inside the big lead dome and eventually you end up in the lantern 200 and odd foot up. The mountaineer appeared at one of the orifices, one of the holes out of the side, there were eight ways out.

The presenter/mountaineer arrives where I am, he's got his microphone with a wire hanging out of it, and he's got his board with all his questions on. I looked at him and said, "Are you coming out on the woodwork to do the interview here?" He said, "Piss off, no way, I'm staying in here".

He did the interview from inside, with me outside, you know, shoving the microphone through the hole to talk to me. The interview went well and I must confess to looking forward to seeing myself on the tele.

You know they always put the idiots on last on the news in case it's all been bad news. Men who think they can fly or men who think they've invented perpetual motion and it's to give you a bit of a laugh in case it's all been miserable bad news you see. Well they put me on at the end on the last three minutes. I enjoyed watching myself on tele, and was very popular for a while, everyone in my area had watched me.

A few days later the phone rang, it was a man from the BBC. "Can I come and see you with a television director" I said, "Yes if you want". I'm an easy going sort of guy like you know. Next day he arrived, when I saw him I thought bloody hell, he looks just like Stewart Grainger, he was six foot tall, all dressed in denim, with a cap with the biggest neb I've ever seen in my life, you know, before they became popular in England, you know one of them big 'uns with a hole in the back, all the kids have got them now, a pair of boots like two canal boats, and he talked in a different language, I didn't understand what he was on about, but we ended up down the pub and I'll never forget the next bit, at the end of the evening I said to him "What do you want me to do? Give you a ring if we're going to do something particularly dangerous or exciting?" and he said, "No don't ring us, we'll ring you", like the proverbial out of work actor sort of thing.

From where I am, I look 200 foot down below at all the little people like cockroaches running about on the precinct.

But being a bit slow like, I realised that he obviously thought that it was a waste of money trying to make a film about a bloody idiot like me.

Anyway he went, normality had nearly come back into my life and people had stopped saying, "I saw you on the news last Thursday" and all that. Then the phone rang again and this lady came on and said, "I work for the BBC". "Can we bob over and see you?", and I said "Aye of course you can".

The woman arrived and brought her boyfriend who was the Director and he was just the same as the other fella but a smaller version, the neb on his cap weren't as big and his boots weren't as big, but he was just as bloody awkward and weird.

By this time I'd had about a month to think about what I would do if they made a film about steeplejacking. The obvious thing to me at least, is you would want to show me putting the ladders up a chimney. From start to finish.

Anyway, I said, "Well I think we should put the ladders up" and he said, "How do you do it" and I said, "Well verbally it's very complicated", I'll show you, so I set off and we got one and a half ladders up a chimney stack and he said "Forget it, it's too technical. They will get bored and turn off, you know. He says we'll bob over next week Jean and see if it's worth it." And they went away with a real nonchalant manner.

Anyway all week I got to thinking about this, I thought I'm going to keep shoving the ladder business and portray how steeplejacks put ladders up the side of a 200 foot pile of bricks with nothing there, only a smooth wall you see.

At the end of the evening but for the grace of God, it nearly never happened...

Next week came, he was just as adamant, and he didn't want to know about me laddering a chimney. At the end of the evening but for the grace of God, it nearly never happened and he muttered something like "Where are you working?", and I said, "Shore near Oldham", which is a little village on the mountains on the outside of the town. It was a particularly beautiful area it had two great big Accrington brick spinning mills 6 storeys high with a 90 foot gap down the middle and a 245 foot chimney with a big top on in the middle and five of my platforms underneath the top, and a railway line, everything was there, all the ingredients for a good Lowry painting.

The backcloth was the bloody Pennine Chain with the sheep farms and the dry stone walls and I'd just got to the top and had a fag and just finished coughing and all that and in they came round the corner in his mini with the arse hanging out of it. They get out; I'm not going down 245 bloody feet, when I've just got to the top. I get on with me job. Ten minutes go by and I look down, he's jumping up and down waving his hands about below so I thought, "Well I'd better go down and see what he wants"?

Anyway I go down and oh he's inspired and says, "Wonderful, wonderful we'll be here in the morning". And that is how it all started.

They made this film and it was supposed to be a 20 minute film that he was going to put on the end of a film called 'Earning a Bob or Two' a series about people like vicars who had a sideline and doctors who did something else and fire brigade and policemen and all that.

The series came and went, they gave me 350 quid, but they just kept coming back and having another go, and said we'll see you next Wednesday and we'll see you in August on the 23rd you know, I've even forgotten when they bloody came.

The films won academy awards and they came back and made another four then they made another five. What I will tell you, is that when the BBC came all those years ago the director had a mini with the arse hanging out of it and when he went away many years later he'd got a brand new bloody Porsche. It's true! And here I am still driving my clapped out Land Rover.

28

THEY ALL CAME TUMBLING DOWN!

Did you know that the BBC Programme "Fred Dibnah Steeplejack"

won a BAFTA award?

by
Fred Dibnah

Then, on the evening of the Awards ceremony, the phone rang, and a very cultured lady from BBC Oxford Road in Manchester said, "I don't know if anyone has told you Fred, but you've been nominated for a Bafta Award this evening. And even if you do not win, it is a high honour to be selected from the many hundreds. You are in the top three".

So, me and Alison sat there at 8.30pm in front of the television and the usual beautiful skinny actress in long black dress with the brown envelope stood in front of the microphone. After her telling us about the other two up for it as well as ours, she ripped the top off the brown paper envelope and says:

"The winner is - Fred Dibnah Steeplejack."

We'd won! WON! Bloody hell, I just could not BELIEVE IT!

Another chap comes over, and he goes "Do you know, you're up for the Academy Awards, Fred?"

It was a bit strange really, because Don Howarth's first series about me was shown on BBC2 in the late seventies - think it were 1978 or summat. Then, within a week or two, they repeated it on BBC1. I'll never forget that night - it was a Friday, and it was my turn to go out for the fish and chips. I thought I'd just call in the Conservative Club and have a quick pint on the way. So, I went in and I'm leaning on the bar having a chat with a mate of mine, who was very generous and bought me a pint. Another chap comes over, and he goes "Do you know, you're up for the Academy Awards, Fred?"

I thought to myself, bloody hell, this feller is taking the Mickey, this lads having a bit of a laugh - but he insisted it was true; he'd read it in a Showbiz journal or whatever. I said I'd never heard of it, but he goes: "There's three documentaries nominated and yours - 'Fred Dibnah Steeplejack' - is up for one of the awards."

I'm now watching the box, looking for Mr Howarth, expecting him to spring up at any moment out of the crowd where they're all sat, with the BBC white wine, frilly shirts and stiff collars. Then they announced "Don Howarth Director"

But he wasn't there! He was in Portugal having a weekend away or summat. They had to give it to someone else on his behalf. But in a few days after he'd got wind of this, he were back again to see me about making some more programmes. One thing I will say about Don, he knew when he was onto a good thing.

THE WAR EFFORT

FRED'S 1927 350CC AJS

BY

FRED DIBNAH

"Um, yeah, me old motor bike, eh? Well, I had to sell it for the war effort when I had me first divorce, you see. It's one of the things I regret most is that, 'avin to let me motorbike go. A beautiful 1927 350cc AJS. I once strapped a bloody great anvil on me back, and rode to me mam's house through the streets of Bolton, wobbling all over the place under the weight of it. Some bloke had sold it to me for a fiver, and I didn't have a motor car to shift it with. I was just getting an unbelievable interest in starting up me blacksmithing around then, and this thing turned up. Aye, I loved that bike... women though; I mean - they cost a lot of pennies them divorces, don't they?"

	Lot Number	Sold for £		Unsold at £
SOTHEBY'S FOUNDED 1744				
34-35 New Bond Street, London W1A 2AA Telephone: 01-493 8080 Telex: 24454 (SPBLON-G) Registered at this address No. 874867	36	1,700.00		
FRED DIBNAH ESQ 121 RADCLIFFE ROAD BOLTON				
Account No. 188778				
The result of your sale of **V & V MOTORBIKES**				
on the 07/10/85 was as detailed				
Commission will be deducted at the rate shown together with any additional charges and a statement of account with proceeds will be sent one month after the sale date.				
	Total sold £ 1,700.00		Total unsold £ 0.00	

The war effort was Fred's divorce from his first wife Alison, and the bike had been sold at Sothebys in October 1985. Twenty years later, it was still a sore point with Fred, who often after a pint or two, especially when looking at vintage motorbikes on some rally, would go into rhetoric about how he would some day buy another one. It wasn't anything to do with possessions, just the pure joy and beauty of the machine. To the mechanically minded Fred, it was like having a bereavement in the family having to part with his treasured bike, and knowing this, fellow like-minded males would often commiserate. Fred did not have a similar attitude for modern vehicles though.

"Me missus has just bought a new shiny car and 'av just dinted the door on the way to' chippy, like. Got into a fair bit of trouble for that, but it doesn't bother me a lot. I've got me lanny, that's alreight, a proper vehicle, you can do a lot of bangin about wi' them, and easily mend owt that goes wrong... but these modern things, well, it's all timing belts and bloody on-board computers or summat. I might buy another motor bike one day. I'm not knackered yet, I could still ride one an' all..."

33

The AJS motorbike was originally brought by Derek Rosco (second hand) for £5 from a Scottish church minister called Duncan McClachlan, Derek had spotted the bike for sale in the advertising section of Motor Sport Magazine. The bike was later purchased by Fred (after much haggling) for 21 guineas. You will notice that on the photos the bike has two different number plates. Fred purchased a dodgy log book from friend Alan Crompton. The log book was for a 250cc bike. By swapping the number plates, Fred could then ride the bike without having to take a motorbike test. Needless to say, he never got caught? The engine shed at Fred's yard that houses his steam engine Caroline was originally purpose built for Fred's AJS motorbike. The windows were constructed so that he could see his pride and joy as he walked past.

Age did not matter to Fred, always young at heart, he had just turned sixty, and with the owner's permission, he jumped onto a vintage motor bike on a steam rally during one summer. Without further ado, he kick-started the machine into action, and immediately shot off across the field in the direction of the arena. For several minutes, he gunned the throttle, gathering speed and amusing the crowds with his antics - losing his flat cap in the process. He returned exhilarated and obviously having enjoyed the experience and some bright spark shouted out *"Did you like that, Fred?"* As he dismounted the machine, he swore he would buy another one day, adding, *"Its magic, they aren't like modern motor cars these y'know, you can work on 'em and 'av a bit of fun, get about a bit... do you wanna sell it mate?"*

"It's magic, they aren't like modern motor cars these y'know, you can work on 'em and 'av a bit of fun, get about a bit... do you wanna sell it mate?"

THE STEAM RALLY SCENE
BY SHEILA DIBNAH

"Is your hobby an extension of your work, then - would you say?" Enquired a keen fan, as Fred signed an autograph for the waiting man in his usual flowing script. "Eh? oh aye, I suppose it is now. Before the telly come along, I never had enough money, you need a lot of green 'uns' for the upkeep of summat like this, you see and ..." Without delay, as to prove his point, Fred gestures towards 'Betsy' with an outstretched arm. Spotting a couple of kids trying to climb up on the front forks of the roller, he stops what he is saying, and instead barks. "Christ! Just a minute mate, them kids have their bloody feet all over me shiny new paintwork..." and at that, jumps up from the plastic chair, nearly tipping over the merchandise-laden table, before dashing off across the grass. "I won't be a minute, mate ..." he salutes the large, waiting queue as he strides purposely off towards his beloved traction engine. People take photographs as he waves his arm at the kids. Another video is sold, with the explanation that it's not been seen on television, the man hands over his £14.99, and says he's been queuing for over half an hour to meet his hero.

It's another day in the life of a famous steeplejack, another steam rally appearance for the mechanical genius. By the time the turn of the century came round, Fred could hardly move for autograph hunters, and people eager to shake his hand whenever he went to such an organised event. But it wasn't always like this, and Fred would often recall happier times, such as the late seventies when he could play to his hearts' content with his roller on such a rally, and drink beer unimpeded with a group of similar-minded friends, conversation centring on engines.

After ridding the engine of muddy kids' feet and stoking the firebox, he returns to the table, and explains, once settled back in the chair, "Hell, before the television came into my life mate, there's no bloody way I'd ever 'av come down this far. I couldn't have afforded to take the time off for one thing. I always used to 'road' me engine to a rally in the good old days, but now it's all low-loader stuff. It'd take you a week to get here!" The 'good old days' of course, to which Fred referred were such steam gatherings as Astle Park in Cheshire.

It would take Fred a couple of days to reach the event, and that to him was part of the fun, stopping at pubs on the way. Fred fondly recalled times when Alison and he would kip down under a flat-bed trailer draped with a tarpaulin. "Yeah, well, I did a lot of boozin' in them days – but it were a lot of fun, not like now when I've got to sit at a table all day and write my name. But that's how it is since the fella came with the magic lantern, that's how I earn me bread and butter. All the factory chimneys are gone anyway."

This particular 'modern day' steam rally was a cracker: The Rushden Cavalcade, at Higham Ferrers in Northamptonshire, and this was our second visit. It was one of Fred's favourites, and he was looking forward to a road run later down to the local village. A marshal, dressed in a yellow vest wanders over and enquires if Fred can have the engine in the area at 2pm, directly after the tractor parade. It's half an hour off and the waiting queue still stretched out endlessly. Someone plonks down another pint of 'Cavalcade Crippler'; a beer specially brewed for the event, on the table in front of Fred, and he takes a long cool draw of the dark, frothy liquid. "By 'eck, bloody good stuff, that!"

Not like this bloody thing here with a top speed of 4 mph and no diff, and if you go over a manhole, you wanna watch where yer bloody tongue is, 'cos you'll bite it off if yer not careful...

2pm arrives, and now the arena, the air redolent with sulphur and black smoke is full of chugging engines led by 'Betsy', the centre of everyone's attention as crowds gather at the perimeter fence. Our hero is speaking over a tinny-sounding tannoy, and several people strain to listen to him over a loud barrel organ, which plays the same tune every half hour. "Next time I'm here, I'll be bringing me tractor along, it's still in me shed in bits, but I intend finishing it, paid over two thousand quid for it I did. That's got springs as well, and it'll do about 15 mph reet comfy-like, and go down hills proper an' all. Not like this bloody thing here with a top speed of 4 mph and no diff, and if you go over a manhole, you wanna watch where yer bloody tongue is, 'cos you'll bite it off if yer not careful..." The crowd laughed. They all love Fred. Listening to a few further tales, they all finally cheer as he waves and climbs back up on the engine to leave the arena after a few laps with the other engines.

This particular 'modern day' steam rally was a cracker: The Rushden Cavalcade, at Higham Ferrers in Northamptonshire

A brief respite for fun, it is back to the table for more autograph signing. Someone else asks about how he got the engine down here, and jokes that Fred can't stop off at pubs on the way down when told about the low loader. Fred looks up seriously, as if recalling some matter of great importance, "Naahh...I gerra bit fed-up at times of all the publicity an' all, but it's an ill wind that blows no bugger any good an' so I've done alreet out of it I suppose. Tell you what though; there were some funny happenings back in them days ..." (muses Fred, almost to himself) "...a mate and me were on't way back home from one particular gathering - think it were Barton Aerodrome or summat – after't first missus had got fed up of all me boozin' on them things an' she'd stopped coming.

A nyway, me mate Mick started to feel a bit poorly, like. Kept rubbing his belly, he looked a bit green round the gills as well. I said 'what's up with yer?' and he said his 'old man' had been givin' him a fair bit o' bother all weekend, and had swollen up to almost twice the size. Poor bugger ended up in agony wi' it and jumped off half way home, sayin' he couldn't stand it no more, and cadged a lift back to Bolton off some bugger in a pub with a red car. When I saw him later that week, I said 'what were up with yer tackle then, eh Mick?' He told me he'd been to see a doctor, and the doctor had examined it and told him ''Well Mr Hobbs, it looks as though you've caught an infection off all the mineral oil during your trip out with Mr Dibnah on the engine." Me mate, bit of a dry bugger at times, had replied "Well doctor – can you possibly do anything to take away the pain, but LEAVE the swelling ...!"

37

NATIONAL JOINT COUNCIL FOR THE BUILDING INDUSTRY

DEED OF APPRENTICESHIP.
FORM No. 1

This Deed of Apprenticeship made the 4th day of October 1954 BETWEEN ---- William Rawlinson --------

of Bk. Boston Street, Halliwell, Bolton in the County of Lancaster (hereinafter called "the Master") of the first part

-------- Frank Dibnah --------

of 8 Alfred Street, Bolton aforesaid

-------- (hereinafter called "the Guardian") of the second part

-------- Frederick Dibnah --------

of 8 Alfred Street, Bolton aforesaid

-------- (hereinafter called "the Apprentice") of the third part

and -------- Arthur Wallwork Talbot --------

of "High-Close", Chorley New Road, Heaton, Bolton aforesaid (hereinafter called "the Representative") of the fourth part.

WHEREAS

(1) The Representative has been selected by the Local Joint Apprenticeship Committee for the Bolton and Farnworth Area of the North Western Region constituted by the National Joint Council for the Building Industry, to be a party to this Deed in accordance with their Scheme of Apprenticeship dated the first day of November, 1945, and

(2) The Apprentice has attained the age of 16 years and is employed on probation by the Master with a view to becoming an apprentice in the Building Industry, and

(3) The Master and the Representative are satisfied that the Apprentice is a suitable person to be taught and instructed as an apprentice in the craft of a Joiner, and

(4) The Guardian and the Representative have enquired into the nature of the business conducted by the Master and desire that the Apprentice should learn the craft of a Joiner in the service of the Master.

NOW THIS DEED WITNESSETH as follows:—

1. The Apprentice of his own free will and with the consent of the Guardian hereby binds himself as Apprentice in the craft of a Joiner and the

IN WITNESS whereof the Common Seal of the party of the first part has hereunto been affixed and the parties of the second third and fourth parts have hereunto set their hands and seals the day and year first above written.

IN WITNESS whereof the parties hereto have hereunto set their hands and seals the day and year first above written.

The Common Seal of _____

_____, Limited,

was hereunto affixed in the presence of

_____

Signed sealed and delivered by the above-named

William Rawlinson

in the presence of *W. Hallinshead*
20 Wood Street,
Bolton.

William Rawlinson
(The Master)

Signed sealed and delivered by the above-named

Frank Dibnah

in the presence of *W. Hallinshead*
20 Wood Street,
Bolton.

Frank Dibnah
(The Parent or Guardian)

Signed sealed and delivered by the above-named

Frederick Dibnah

in the presence of *W. Hallinshead*
20 Wood Street,
Bolton.

Frederick Dibnah
(The Apprentice)

Signed sealed and delivered by the above-named

Arthur Wallwork Talbot

in the presence of *W. Hallinshead*
20 Wood Street,
Bolton.

J. F. Talbot
(The Representative)

Endorsement of Deed of Apprenticeship

A. We (i) the Master and (ii) the Representative hereby certify that this Deed of Apprenticeship terminated on the *28th April 1959.* has been faithfully complied with and is hereby endorsed in accordance with the provisions of Clause 2(k) thereof.

(i) *William Rawlinson* Master.
(ii) *J F Bolton* Representative.

B. We further certify that during the period of apprenticeship the Apprentice_____
_____ has attained the following awards :—

(i) _____
(ii) _____
(iii) _____
(iv) _____
(v) _____

THE PEAK FOREST DISASTER
WHEN THINGS GO WRONG

Somewhere under the layers of undercoat and green paint on the right hand side of Fred's living wagon you will find the story of The Peak Forest Disaster. It was Midsummer's day July 1986.

These pictures tell a story all of their own. It was an incident that the usually very talkative Fred didn't like to speak about. We have searched our archive, looked in books, listened to hours of after dinner talks and stage shows, asked friends and steam men. But drawn a blank. So we must assume that this encounter truly rattled Fred to the point where his lips were sealed forever.

The Peak Forest Disaster

Fred Dibnah Aveling & Porter Steam Roller ran away backwards down Mount Pleasant Hill Peak Forest Derbyshire on Midsummer's day 1986

The Living van turned over - there were no fatalities
Repairs were carried out in the Devonshire Arms car park
Peak Forest 1986

Sue Lorenz - Steerswoman

Bernard Barker Joiner/publican

Frank Hardman Stopper Upper

Fred Dibnah
The man who did all the damage
1986

The photo right tells the story

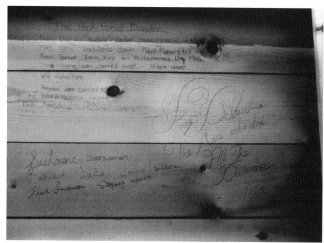

BETSY

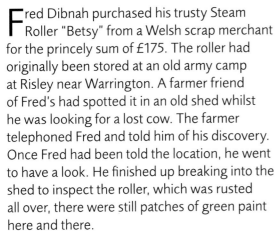

Fred Dibnah purchased his trusty Steam Roller "Betsy" from a Welsh scrap merchant for the princely sum of £175. The roller had originally been stored at an old army camp at Risley near Warrington. A farmer friend of Fred's had spotted it in an old shed whilst he was looking for a lost cow. The farmer telephoned Fred and told him of his discovery. Once Fred had been told the location, he went to have a look. He finished up breaking into the shed to inspect the roller, which was rusted all over, there were still patches of green paint here and there.

The roller has had two names whilst in Fred's custody. The first name was Alison after Fred's first wife, but after their divorce Fred renamed the engine "Betsy" after his mother. The reason for this he would say "Mothers are always constant and reliable".

THE STORY OF MR. BONGABOO
BY PAUL DONOGHUE

It all seems like such a long time ago. I often wonder if it really happened. Did I really spend several months filming Fred Dibnah?

When I knew him, he was well known in his local area far more than he was nationally. People would point at him and say, look that's Fred Dibnah from the telly. But never in my wildest dreams did I ever think that this little feller from Bolton would become a world famous TV personality, a Doctor, a Member of the British Empire and a much loved international icon.

I will always remember my first telephone conversation with Fred. I had watched him on the telly and noticed that there were no videos about him in the market place. I thought I would contact his agent and see if there could be an opportunity to film him knocking down a chimney or two, and film him out with his traction engine or maybe spend some time filming in his steam powered workshop and yard.

I rang the BBC in London; I was amazed when they said they had never heard of him.

How do you contact someone like Fred Dibnah? I rang the BBC in London; I was amazed when they said they had never heard of him. I was passed to several departments who were clueless as to who I was talking about. I then rang some high profile entertainment agencies. Fred who? They couldn't help either. In desperation I tried directory enquiries (in the days when you dialled 192 and it cost 10 pence for 2 name searches). I knew they wouldn't have his number, but it was worth a shot (if they did have the number I was expecting it to be ex-directory).

"Do you have a number for a Fred Dibnah in Bolton Lancashire?"

"How are you spelling the surname?"

"It's D I B N A H."

"Oh the chimney man who was on BBC2 last night?"

"Yes that's right."

(Slight pause as she tapped on her computer). "Yes sir, that's 0204 31303."

I was completely taken aback, was this really going to be this simple? I then went into a five minute conversation with the directory enquiries lady who turned out to be a true fan of Fred's.

Armed with the information, I picked up the receiver, dialled the number and took a deep breath. The phone rang about 10 times and then it was answered. Before I could say a word this deep Bolton accent said, "You'll have to speak up, I'm deaf in one ear and we have got steam up in me shed - boiler inspector is coming next week so we're having a trial run".

So shouting down the phone I said, "Is that Fred Dibnah?"

"What? I can't hear you cock speak up."

"IS THAT FRED DIBNAH?"

"Aye cock it is, I've got steam up and it's bloody noisy in here, and I can't hear a thing."

"Fred I'm Paul Donoghue and I want to make a video about you."

"What did you say cock?"

"I SAID I'M PAUL DONOGHUE AND I WANT TO MAKE VIDEO ABOUT YOU."

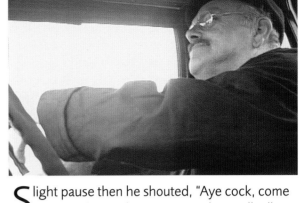

Slight pause then he shouted, "Aye cock, come down to the yard tomorrow and we will talk about it over a brew, about 10ish". Then silence. He'd hung up? I sat at my desk scratching my head. It was one of those "did that really happen?" moments. I was just glad I lived in Rotherham and not on the Isle of Wight.

"You'll have to speak up, I'm deaf in one ear and we have got steam up in me shed - boiler inspector is coming next week so we're having a trial run"

Next morning I was up bright and early, I had a nice leisurely drive to Bolton. (This was in a time when you could drive on the motorways with very few hold ups). I found Radcliffe Road easily - not by using a map or planning my route, I just wound my window down when I got to Bolton and asked a passer by.

"Do you know where Fred Dibnah lives?"

"Aye cock, you go down there, through the lights, keep going till you see the garage on the right then turn right just before it."

The job was simple and my luck was in, I had taken the right turn off the bypass and I was very close to my destination.

I turned onto Radcliffe Road and on my left I could see these green railings that stretched for 75 yards or so. I pulled up next to the gates and parked behind a green living van and got out of the car (it was 5 to 10). Suddenly a Land Rover groaned up the drive covered in ladders and ropes and pulleys, etc. It was Fred.

"All right cock; you must be Paul Bongaboo."

"Its Paul Donoghue actually."

"Aye cock, jump in. She who must be obeyed has run out of milk. No milk no brew." (It was a bit like a Wallace and Grommet sketch). I walked round to the passenger seat of the Land Rover, opened the door and there in the foot-well was a little ginger haired lad about 3 or 4 years old. "Shift over Jack and sit on Mr Bongaboo's knee."

Suddenly a Land Rover groaned up the drive covered in ladders and ropes and pulleys, etc. It was Fred. "All right cock; you must be Paul Bongaboo."

"It's Paul Donoghue actually."

"Aye cock jump in."

So we're off to god knows where, everyone we passed was waving to Fred as we drove down the roads. Fred starts; "I've got a boiler inspection next week and I'm in a bit of a panic. See I've been running me yard without a certificate and someone's reported me, it will be one of those bloody environmentalists you can bet." Jack is hanging out of the passenger window singing, "Row, row, row your boat gently down the stream. Merrily, merrily, merrily, merrily, life is but a dream." His little boots are covered in oil, grease and grime. My trousers were soon filthy, I was not impressed.

We pull up at a local corner shop and Fred jumps out. He gets a chock out of the back of the Land Rover and puts it under the driver's wheel, he sticks his head through the driver's window and says to me, "Hand brake's knackered pal, sometimes it just goes without warning." He then speaks to Jack who is now sat in the driver's seat. "Listen me little mate, you stop here with Paul Bong a Boo while I go and get some milk for a brew." Jack jumps straight out of the car, slams the door and gives me a 'I'm not stopping with you' look. He slips his little hand into his Dads and they enter the shop.

So here I am sat in an oil covered Land Rover with light trousers on and a white shirt. Jack has buggered my clothes and I look like I've been down a mine. I'm thinking Fred hasn't got a clue who I am or what I have come for. Plus we were parked on a hill with a dodgy hand break. I was not amused by my situation.

Ten minutes go by and people are stopping to look around the Land Rover. Heads are poking inside, it's like I'm not there. I'm just hoping no-one kicks the chock. I wasn't in the mood for travelling towards Bolton backwards in a Land Rover with 20 ladders on it, and no brakes!

Twenty minutes go by, then thirty minutes. I have seen people going in the shop, but no-one's coming out. I get out of the Land Rover and walk to the door of the shop. There are 30 people in there listening to Fred Dibnah telling a tale.

Fred's arms are going up and down as he tells his story. "I grabbed me jack hammer, as cracks were going up this chimney 10 foot at a time, bricks are falling off, the roar of the fire, she's going" everyone in the shop is mesmerised by Fred's story, he's telling the puddle story (which I later timed at 12 minutes).

I have now walked in the shop and am listening intently (there is a smile on my face, this is a funny story). It then dawned on me that Jack, Fred and I are the only white people in the shop, Fred is telling this tale to a shop full of his local Asians. They were loving it and hanging on every word. Fred would have gone down well in Islamabad.

Arms are still swinging. "I shout to Donald, run Donald she's going to go, then whoosh I'm up to my chest in water. I look up and I think, I'm going to die." Everyone in the shop is spellbound, still hanging on every word.

Fred takes another 10 minutes to complete the gripping tale. Then he says to the shop keeper, "Bloody hell, I've left Mr Bong a Boo in me truck outside. I forgot all about him. I'll catch you later cock."

Fred then walked out of the shop followed by everyone who had been listening to the tale. As he told his tale, Fred hadn't noticed me behind the rack of Walkers crisps. As I walked out of the shop Fred said to Jack, "Bloody hell mate he's gone".

That was how it all started and I am honoured that I now have the opportunity to recount three of my own special personal stories in this wonderful publication.

RAF Burtonwood was probably the largest military base in Europe during World War II, processing over 11,500 aircraft between 1943 and 1945 alone, but beyond that it was responsible for the support of initially the 8th Air Force, then additionally the 9th and ultimately the 12th and 15th Air Forces as well. Steeplejacks Fred Dibnah and Eddy Chattwood arrived at Burtonwood in April 1988 under contract to Atherton Demolition. The Control Tower stood on six reinforced concrete legs, each being 18 inches square. 3 legs were carefully removed using 6 inch steel mesh rock drills and a gas axe to burn away the metal reinforcements. Each leg was supported by 4 telegraph poles. Eddy Chattwood says that he and Fred had to work in very windy conditions and were both spooked by the constant banging of corrugated metal sheets and the howling wind. "It was like we weren't meant to be there and was very scary" he said. On the day of the drop 3 big fires had to be lit and within 23 minute the structure collapsed to the ground. As the tower fell a family of resident ducks flew out of a midway window. Eddy says that after the drop Atherton Demolition invited everyone to hospitality at a pub that was decorated like a wedding reception. Eddy said "The only thing missing was the Bride and Groom, but it was a free bar". Eddy Chattwood worked with Fred Dibnah from 1968 onwards, and assisted on many of Fred's early demolition jobs.

FRED DIBNAH TO AIR TRAFFIC CONTROL

49

TOOLS OF THE TRADE

FRED AND HIS LAND ROVERS

.... Like really, I've never owned a motor vehicle ... well, I have I suppose, I once owned a 1927 Rover. But it were no good; everything was wrong with it – the back axle was goosed, and the engine block were cracked – and it had various other faults. Well, I really wanted a steam engine anyway, so I flogged it!

Anyway, the first thing I ever had with four wheels was an ex-WD Land Rover. I paid £425 for it – and it was taxed and insured, ready for the road. And it was all painted up nice and green, and had been done up by a good man, who to this day, still specialises in rejuvenated ex-WD.

That one lasted me for a long time. It was rather strange, because it was about five or six years earlier when I passed my driving test – and I'd never since been behind the wheel of anything. I went for this thing, and I'd got to drive it home, which was quite a hairy experience. My driving skills have not really improved a lot, actually!

The thing is - life went by, of course. My idea of maintenance of motor vehicles is nil! I just treated it as a tool. Got out of bed in a morning, pressed the button and it went 'whooomph' – and off it went.

The first ailments, like flat batteries, and things like that, and broken half-shafts with putting too much weight on it – expecting too much over what the thing was designed for – crippled it in the end; it was the excessive weight that I put on it. All the time, I am struggling hard to earn a living, with the steeplejacking, and I could never aspire to a brand-new one.

What always used to upset me immensely was seeing a brand-new Land Rover, with a woman in it – handbag on the seat – and that were it! Somebody told me a tale quite recently, about going down the road with a trailer on the back of their vehicle, and being met by somebody – a lady – with a four-wheel drive Land Rover. She refused to leave the road because of the muck at the side of the road – and she was driving a bloody vehicle designed for ploughing across fields!

The thing is - the first Land Rover; I had many traumas – I remember coming back home one day, down the drive, which is quite steep. I put the brakes on – nothing happened... I grabbed hold of the hand brake – nothing! It carried on proceeding down the hill, through a holly bush, and finally came to rest on the lawn in the middle of the garden. It had the half-shaft sticking out, with a wheel on the end of it! That was disaster number one...

The other frightening thing was - I went to see one of my friends who lived in the country. On the way back, there was an unbelievable rattling which started up. I got home, came down the drive again, and swung the thing round the ash tree at the bottom. I put the brakes on, and the front right-hand corner proceeded to collapse on to the floor! All the wheel nuts had pulled through the hub at the centre of the wheel. Bloody wheel fell off! Anyway, that was the end of that.

The last and final straw with the Land Rover – I came steaming in again, put the brakes on – a big cloud of cream smoke came from under the bonnet. I lifted the bonnet, and the whole electrical system was glowing red...and it bursts into flames... it never went again after that!

So, by this time I had succumbed to a lightweight version. The finances were slightly better by now and I had it painted in Holland's Meat Pie colours. It was dark green at the bottom, and a red seven-inch wide strip down the middle, and then dark brown at the top. And splendid gold lettering on it: 'F. Dibnah Steeplejack'. It looked really beautiful; but it was a bit hard work getting the ladders on the top of it. The other thing – they tell me these Land Rover men – that these light-weight things were never as well designed as the ordinary ones, because they were designed for dropping out of aeroplanes. Even though this machine looked very well; I think they'd dropped it out of one-too-many aeroplanes, because it were never any bloody good! Finally, the chassis broke in half, and I sold it for a hundred quid...

Then I got one that I thought would last me through until my retirement, which I'm just now three years short of. Here again, the maintenance aspect of it weren't up to much... I put the petrol in, the oil in and water in the radiator. I did some fairly big jobs with that. I mended two steam engines. I dismantled the steam engines, and brought them long distances. Of course, when you load a Land Rover up, it decimates the steering gear. Coming down the motorway, with the front end drifting across the road – makes it very difficult to control. This happens when you are grossly overloaded at the arse-end, you know, the spring's the other way up! Anyway, this went on...then the rust starts, and you need another patch on the chassis. Then another. Then the bulkhead rotted away.

Then... an unbelievable stroke of luck! A man called Chris Crane rang up from a company called RPI Engineering, in Norfolk. He's seen it on the telly programmes, racing reputedly from one end of England to the other. We only went about a few hundred yards away from home, and rode up and down the motorway a million times, with the camera in all sorts of positions – and up over the moors. We broke the shock absorbers on the T.V. director's car - but it didn't do any harm to the Land Rover - it ploughed on over all this rough tract up near the T.V. mast on top of Winter Hill! It was supposed to be over Dartmoor or somewhere on the series.

51

Anyway, Chris had seen it on telly. He said "If you let me convert your Land Rover to gas, I'll do it for nothing!" I said "Hang on mate, you know, this bloody vehicle is something else - when you are going along the road in the pouring rain and you go through a puddle, you've got to have your wellies on; there's no bottom in it, like!"

The engine's goosed, the gearbox is knackered – and I only had one windscreen wiper. The other one, I'd converted it to 'handraulic'... I had a lever inside the cab that you worked. In heavy showers, you'd got to get hold of this handle, and pull it. It was like the very earliest form of windscreen wiper. It was easier than trying to find one that worked.

Anyway, he was bent on doing this job, and kept ringing up about it. I tried to put him off, but finally, I succumbed to his request. One Sunday, the man arrived in a more-or-less brand-new Range Rover, gas-fired, closely followed by John Bolt, a writer from one of the Land Rover magazines. He arrived in a brand-new light blue Land Rover - hammer finish – gas fired. It had all these things that I dream about! Soon after, another man turned up, driving a long wheelbase ex-WD one, with a rag roof. Three Land Rovers, and my clapped-out one!

The engine's goosed, the gearbox is knackered – and I only had one windscreen wiper. The other one, I'd converted it to 'handraulic'... I had a lever inside the cab that you worked.

"Do you think it will make it, back to Norfolk?" I said, "Well, if I were driving it; yeah, yeah – but I wouldn't go above fifty-odd mile an hour.

Chris surveyed it – it didn't look too bad – but you couldn't really see underneath. When you looked at the bulk-head, and the rot; the hinges just about holding on to the side...various other things, like bent bumpers and bad bumps in it, where things had hit it on demolition sites – all of that. It's had a few bricks land on it, on odd occasions!

He said "Do you think it will make it, back to Norfolk?" I said, "Well, if I were driving it; yeah, yeah – but I wouldn't go above fifty-odd mile an hour. At that speed, its O.K. Might be a bit noisy, smoky and uncomfortable, but it won't give up. It keeps going."

So he hung about for about two hours and finally decided he'd have a go at driving it back to Norfolk. He bid us good day, and set off. My day wore on in the back yard. Being a bit deaf, I have the bell off a fire engine in my workshop, with a string to the back kitchen. About half-past seven, my wife Sheila pulled the string, and rung the bell. When I appeared out of the shed door, she said:

"The man from Norfolk's just been on..."
"What did he say?"
" Well, I went: do you want a word with Fred?"
And he carried on "No, I feel ill and I'm knackered. All the noise and the smoke – I need to rest – I just thought I'd let you know it made it here, tell him I'll ring him next week...!"

So next week came, and about Thursday, the telephone rang. It was Chris. He said, "Well, I've got some bad news – the engine is no good. It's not worth repairing. I'm going to put you a V8 in instead." I thought – bloody hell! I knew it was too good to be true; I knew it would cost me summat! He said "Oh no, I said I'll do it – it won't cost you owt".

Months and months went by, and we had started by this time filming for the new series 'Magnificent Monuments' (more about that later). The Director wanted the vehicle back to do some of the shots, but we hadn't got it!

On one occasion whilst filming, we were up in Edinburgh Castle. This old Darby and Joan couple came up to me "Oh – hello, its Fred isn't it!" They went on "They've got your Land Rover in a garage next door to our house, and they've pulled it into a million pieces. There's nothing left of it, only two rusty girders and four wheels!"

Then the man from Norfolk rang up when I'd returned to Bolton and said, "Really, you know – I've chewed a bit too much off. This chassis – it's had it, beyond repair!" He went on he'd put out on the internet to other Land Rover dealerships and what have you, part mart makers, all of that for a new chassis. He succeeded in getting one; he got a brand-new heavy-duty galvanised chassis, made in Stockport by a man called Mr Marsland.

Then, the rebuilding with the V8 engine commenced. In the end, when desperation had set in to get it back, it was still unfinished. I rang him one day to ask how it was going, and told him the Director wanted it back for the filming.

Anyway, one weekend, they brought it. I must say, it looked very splendid and nice and shiny. It looked like brand-new, but old fashioned. Just the job! But the thing is, this V8 engine is more like a formula one racing car. At the traffic lights, it takes off like buggery. Also, the petrol consumption's doubled!

The bloody sad thing is though, it didn't get back in time to be included in the new set of filming, so we had to use footage of the last stuff filmed for 'Industrial Age' instead. A great pity that, but no doubt it will be included in the next programmes if there are any...'

"They've got your Land Rover in a garage next door to our house, and they've pulled it into a million pieces. There's nothing left of it, only two rusty girders and four wheels!"

Fred Dibnah Visits "The Great Dorset Steam Fair"
by Paul Donoghue

It was after Fred had dropped a chimney at Farnworth that I asked him if he would like to visit The Great Dorset Steam Fair. The yearly event is held on 600 acres of farmland on the outskirts of a village called Tarrant Hinton near Blandford, Dorset. The Steam Fair has the reputation of being the biggest steam event in the world. At its height The Great Dorset Steam Fair would attract almost a quarter of a million visitors and exhibitors, which is the equivalent of a small town of people descending on the area. Fred said, "I don't know if I can go cock, you see, her who must be obeyed has the diary, and Dorset's bloody miles away". I said to Fred that if he could come that I would pay all his petrol, food, beer and a caravan on the site for him to sleep in etc. Looking back, how could our hero possibly refuse? I didn't get an answer straight away, it was obvious that Fred was working on the wife and playing the slowly slowly catch a monkey game.

Several weeks went by and The Great Dorset Steam Fair was getting closer. Fred was having a steam day at Glynllifon Parc in Wales, where he had totally restored a Beam engine. I was driving Fred there in my car and mentioned en route, that I had spoken to Michael Oliver (organiser of The Great Dorset Steam Fair) and he said that if Fred came he would lay on a top of the range caravan for him in the best caravan area on the site, and he would put it near the entrance to the Beer Tents and the Fair. Fred then sat bolt upright and said, " didn't I tell you cock, we're going, that's been decided over a month, bloody hell cock, me brains turning to mash, thought I'd told you? I just hope it doesn't rain like last time I went there, it was like 6 inches of Aero milk chocolate, and it was that bad you couldn't get to the beer tent. My roller never moved in fact nothing really moved; it was what they call one of those disasters". I was amazed that Fred hadn't told me he was coming to Dorset, but you can imagine my delight that he was?

"I don't know if I can go cock, you see, her who must be obeyed has the diary, and Dorset's bloody miles away"...

I made the long drive to The Great Dorset Steam Fair a couple of days before it was due to start, I wanted to make sure that everything was going to run smoothly. I saw Michael Oliver who was busy organising everyone. I had learnt the previous year that Michael Oliver has an ethos of running events all of his own. His complaints procedure is second to none. For instance if a man were to have a complaint and say "Michael someone has set up their stall on my pitch" Michael would say, "I'm just sorting this feller out over here and I will come over to you in 10 minutes". The man with the complaint walks away, because he knows everything will be sorted out.

Meanwhile Michael Oliver jumps in his car and drives half a mile to the other side of the massive site and has breakfast. I was once interviewing Michael and asked him why he did this? His answer was a belter? "I aint got no time to sort out 300 problems at once, people have a funny way of sorting things out themselves, everyone here is a showman of some description, and who can blame them for wanting to be at the front or pinching a bit of someone's plot? When I go home from here, my head hits the pillow and I'm straight to sleep. If I was to take on 300 problems at once, I'd be in the bloody river by March?

Later that day, I did have a complaint of my own; the top of the range caravan turned out to be a two wheeled 3 berth scrapper that looked like it had been saved from a November the 5th bonfire party. It was terrible, covered in mildew and a wreck of the highest proportions. Could I really allow the great Fred Dibnah to reside in such a vehicle?

I marched over to Michael Oliver, "Bloody hell Michael I thought you said top of the range!" "It's an absolute bloody wreck and a disgrace". Michael gave me a sheepish look, he said, "I'm sorry Paul someone must have bloody cocked it up, I'll find out who is responsible and I will be over in 10 minutes, rest assured this will be sorted out, I told them it was for Fred Dibnah!" Michael Oliver then vanished, (a little quicker than usual) he was obviously doing one of his half mile specials. Do I have to finish this story?

58

I spent the rest of the day scrubbing that caravan, buying pillows, air fresheners, towels, carpets, pots, pans etc. I was absolutely incensed. How could this happen to me? Over a few hours it dawned on me. People really do have a funny way of sorting things out themselves. Michael was right! I had turned a wreck of a caravan into an average dwelling. The caravan looked a 100 per cent better than when I had first seen it.

Fred arrived at the event a couple of days later with wife No2. I showed them to their caravan expecting world war three to break out. Fred just stepped into the caravan scratched his chin and made himself comfortable. I came back 10 minutes later and over a brew he asked me what was the running order for filming, and what time did I need him in the morning? He never once mentioned that the caravan was a wreck. I can only assume that on the way to Wales, I had spoken into his deaf ear?

On the first morning of filming Fred was up bright and early, I drove to his location and he was having a wash and a shave on a table outside the caravan. It has always amazed me that when Fred has his cap off nobody recognised him. Steam and Fred Dibnah fans would walk past him and not have a clue as to who he was! Stick his cap and glasses on, and a crowd would develop in minutes.

Fred's first encounter of the morning was with (the late) Jack Wharton. Jack was a marvellous character and I had filmed and interviewed him many times. Fred and Jack were giggling about Dr Giles Romanies having to attend to a patient in the middle of the night and the fact that the good Doctor was dressed like Rip Van Winkle as he scurried in the night.

Jack Wharton was one of the founding members of the National Traction Trust; he was a former president who was held in very high regard by every steam man, when Jack spoke people listened. He was also an accomplished engineer and knew the workings of Steam and Traction Engines inside out.

Our next stop was Chris Edmond's Pilgrim Steam Railway. Fred and Chris were getting on like a house on fire, talking about the old days and the history of the miniature steam railway. Fred loved the little railway and couldn't wait to take the controls himself. As I remember it Fred drove the engine for over half an hour, much to the delight of the fast growing queue of passengers.

It was at this stage that I realized that I could have made a huge mistake and a catastrophic error in judgment. I had brought Fred to one of the biggest events in the country where thousands of members of the public wanted to be near the celebrity. You could hear it, " FRED DIBNAH IS OVER THERE". As we tried to make our film, people totally ignored us but they would clamber to get near Fred. "Can you just sign this programme Fred, make it to aunt Daisy". "Can we have a photo Fred"? Fred, will you say "Did you like that" for my dad, he's always wanted to hear it live. Then the press came, over here Fred, smile Fred, look that way Fred look this way Fred. As the day wore on you could see that Fred was getting fed up. "Bloody hell Paul" he said, "I've never signed so many autographs in my life, I've got writers cramp".

It was at this stage that I realized that I could have made a huge mistake and a catastrophic error in judgment.

We talked about things that evening and decided that we would start earlier (8am), and finish at 1pm. between 11am and 1pm we would have Fred signing autographs at our trade stand. After 1pm Fred was free to do what he liked.

I caught up with Fred late one afternoon having a pint in one of the smaller beer tents. Fred had taken off his cap and was enjoying some peace and quiet. This old chap walked up to me, he had 3 cameras round his neck, plus a variety of lenses etc. He said in a posh voice. "I've been told that Fred Dibnah is somewhere round here, could you possibly direct me to him". Fred lifted his finger to his lips. So I said, "you've just missed him sir, he's gone to the other side of the site looking for Michael Oliver". After he had scurried off, Fred and I had a two hour session sampling the delights of a master brewer. We giggled, laughed and enjoyed each others company. For the first time since Fred had arrived at the Great Dorset Steam Fair he was at peace with himself, and very relaxed.

The stories he told, the knowledge he passed to me, plus the pure delight of being with a genius made all my worry's and troubles of a true filming disaster go away.

I never managed to collect enough footage to make a one hour programme, the end result was a small film of Fred at The Great Dorset Steam Fair, which we included in our master production (simply called) The Great Dorset Steam Fair.

Fred lifted his finger to his lips. So I said, you've just missed him sir, he's gone to the other side of the site looking for Michael Oliver.

Weather Vanes
A Nice Little Hobby

by Sheila Dibnah

Fred had the ultimate recycling idea for old copper hot water cylinders – they ended up as weathervanes!

Most of his weathervanes were made from copper and brass found in a local scrap yard; but his favourite, which he produced for the Stornaway Ferry Terminal in 1996, was constructed from pure stainless steel. Whatever the materials used, the product was the same; a beautiful, highly crafted piece of structural design, suitable to grace any public building with pride. Not all Fred's weathervanes were for the public sector however, private individuals would also commission him to produce vanes, sometimes to their own specification, but more usually the famous cockerel design we are so familiar with from watching him making them on television are what appealed best.

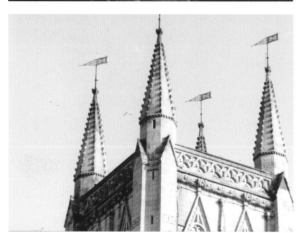

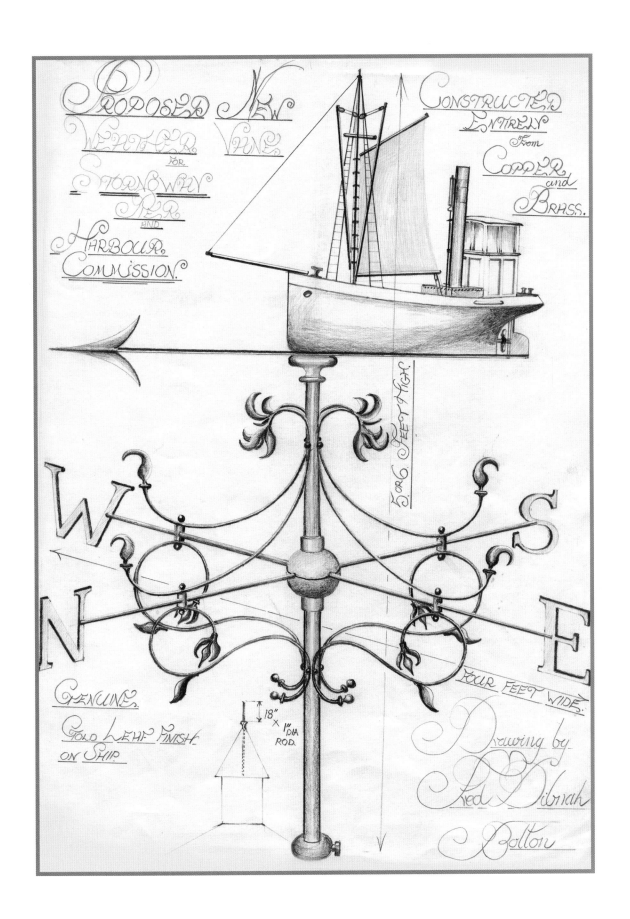

PROPOSED NEW WEATHER VANE FOR STORNOWAY PIER AND HARBOUR, COMMISSION.

CONSTRUCTED ENTIRELY FROM COPPER AND BRASS.

5 OR 6 FEET HIGH.

W N S E

FOUR FEET WIDE.

GENUINE. GOLD LEAF FINISH ON SHIP.

18" × 1" DIA ROD.

Drawing by Fred Dibnah Bolton

65

The price of these varied, but generally, he would ask somewhere in the region of £2,000. If you think about the sheer amount of work involved, both design and practical, they represented very good value indeed. Fred never did them just for the money of course. He was an artist, and the fun was in the great attention to details he gave to each vane, turning it into a true work of art. You only had to watch the loving way in which he applied the gold leaf towards the end of the process to realise this. Being a highly practical man, one of the things he liked about the vanes was their usefulness as well as their decorative purpose.

For the design, Fred would use thin plywood cut into shapes with a jig-saw as patterns to fashion the flattened sheet copper of a water cylinder into the various parts. He would then bend the copper cut-outs and solder the seam to form the body of the cockerel, and seal the broad end (or 'arse-end' as Fred always referred to it) with a concave copper 'lid'. The neck and head of the cockerel were similarly formed into a tube from copper, topped off with a brass head (usually a doorknob or something similar). More wood patterns were used in the same way, enabling Fred to cut the N S E W letters and the wattles, comb and tail of the cockerel from waste sheet brass.

A 'boss' made of solid brass, turned on a lathe and usually stamped with the inscription 'Fred Dibnah & Sons, Bolton' supported the four arms bearing the letters, which were made also from brass.

The whole thing when finished and installed rotated in situ on its axis..... a humble marble! Fred had discovered that marbles were impervious to weather conditions, and the cock could freely move around in the wind for many years without any maintenance.

It was sad that Fred did not manage to make many vanes in his final years, but he always said that he would carry on doing them after finishing his engine. In the shed, to this day, awaits several cockerel heads waiting for their pride of place as part of one of his resplendent weathervanes, complete with all the patterns needed for the job.

It is not clear how many weathervanes Fred produced in his life, but as his fame on television increased, so did demand for them. It was sad that Fred did not manage to make many vanes in his final years, but he always said that he would carry on doing them after finishing his engine. In the shed, to this day, awaits several cockerel heads waiting for their pride of place as part of one of his resplendent weathervanes, complete with all the patterns needed for the job.

THE LAST CHIMNEY IN FARNWORTH

Demolition expert and television celebrity, Fred Dibnah brought down the house when he felled the last standing 19th century red bricked chimney in Farnworth. The site of the BPC works had suffered fire damage and it was decided on safety grounds that the chimney should be demolished. As well as clearing the way for improvements the demolition means that nearby residents will not have to be disturbed by traffic. A new road will be built where the chimney once stood and cars can avoid Mather Street in the future.

Fred said, "This is a beautiful example of a chimney, lovely red brick and in good condition. It's a shame you cant just lift them up and put them somewhere else.

Chairman of BPC said Mike Wilson said " Fred got it right first time, the chimney fell down where it was supposed to. But I must admit I did have my fingers crossed at the time". Locals and television crews gathered to see the stack fall and according to Fred the job went smoothly. "Not a hitch"

67

ALWAYS IN THE PAPERS

BY SHEILA DIBNAH

BiG chimneys

MR. F. DIBNAH, whose home address is 8 Alfred-st. (near Burnden Park), writes to us from Germany, where he is at present doing his National Service, asking for some details about chimneys.

Hardly surprising that he should ask about chimneys for he is a steeplejack in civil life! Mr. Dibnah writes: "Can you tell me something about some old chimneys, such as Dobson's, or the one at Barrow Bridge?"

He also asks did Bolton ever have the biggest chimney in the country. So far as can be traced we never had the country's biggest chimney, but for many years the tallest stack in Lancashire was at Dobson and Barlow's Kay-st. works—367½ft high. For years people argued that it's height was 369½ft. Then Joe Smith, a local steeplejack, climbed up with a tape-measure! After hours of patient measuring he came to earth to announce that the height was exactly 367½ft—and that was that!

Barrow Bridge chimney was formerly 306ft in height, but in 1929 it was reduced to 288ft. Then in 1945 a crack appeared in the fabric so another 36ft. was taken off, making the chimney a mere 252ft.

Where else could you find such an unlikely celebrity as Fred? What was his broad appeal? Certainly, he was a walking encyclopaedia on our industrial heritage. Not to mention all aspects of engineering and steam - but what was the exact magic formula that kept us glued to the box whenever he was on. Why did we love him standing at the side of a grimy factory chimney with a mad grin on his face, turning to the camera, chirping, "Did yer like that?"

His ultimate goal as a young man was to mend the town hall clock in Bolton, and at the age of 25 he had achieved it. Then, the television came along and catapulted him to fame, and perhaps as he always maintained, cost him his marriage, which greatly hurt him.

In 1996 he was approached to take part in an interview for a book called 'The 7 Keys of Charisma' by author Joanna Kozubska, it was surprising to read a passage in which our hero says he often felt a failure. A natural born orator, Fred was also sensitive in many ways, and it is this sensitivity and passion for what he believed in that made him real to the viewing public.

The media loved Fred. So open, honest and sincere, nothing would be off limits. Which other celebrity would tell a reporter all about emotional and financial problems, then add, "Eh, y'won't put all that down, will yer?" It was so typical of him, and as his national fame and popularity grew, fans would identify with the iconic Fred, because of this openness.

Somehow, despite his brilliant talent as an intuitive engineer, artist, demolition and steam expert, television celebrity and all round larger-than-life character, he still managed to retain his 'ordinary bloke' appeal. He could have been your granddad, or the bloke next door who you see down the pub on a Friday night.

You never read anything bad about Fred in the newspapers. He lived life in his own way, and did not mind sharing it. He saw nothing wrong in baring his soul. That is why we all loved Fred - he was one of us.

■ Pride before the fall: Fred with one he didn't blow u

Blast it! Fred drops bricks a day early

BRITAIN'S best-known steeplejack Fred Dibnah has blown his latest project.

TV crews and photographers were invited to watch the Bolton blaster drop a 450ft chimney at Canvey Island, Essex, today.

But 57-year-old Fred went "a tiny bit too far" as he prepared the base and the whole lot fell down 23 hours early.

Only other workers on the former oil refinery site were there to see the concrete chimney's sudden collapse.

After the job was suddenly over Fred said: "It was my decision whether

By Roger Williams

to nibble a bit more out of it or not. It's not a precis science and we went a tin bit too far. This is the firs time we have ever los one."

The chimney was on th site of a new Safewa store, due to open nex month.

Gordon Wotherspoon Safeway managing direc tor for property, said: "W are all pleased that n injuries were caused an the end result wa achieved — albeit a da early.

"Personally, my sympa thies are with Fred."

Bolton steeplejack Fred Dibnah with the unenviable job of removing the cross from the church tower.

Wind damaged cross is hauled down

A LANDMARK in the Tonge Fold area of Bolton for the past 35 years was taken down today.

For the metal cross on top of St Chad's Church was dislodged by high winds at the week-end. One arm of the cross was broken off.

Firemen were called out by the vicar, the Rev Colin Shaw, after the cross was seen hanging precariously down the side of the church's 70ft tower.

Steeplejack

Part of the footpath below was roped off after firemen checked the cross. Today a steeplejack was working on the tower to remove it.

The cross, which was erected with the church in 1939, was illuminated until the past few years, when maintenance and replacement costs proved prohibitive.

Said Mr Shaw: "I don't think it will be put back up now. Even though it is ornamental, it is too expensive to illuminate it or replace parts."

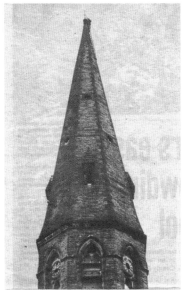

Fred's lovebird rescue mission

By JENNIFER BRADBURY

STEEPLEJACK-cum-television raconteur Fred Dibnah took a step back in time yesterday when he returned to climb his first-ever chimney.

The opportunity to rescale the 262ft Barrow Bridge chimney came about because the RSPB is trying to encourage a pair of rare peregrine falcons to set up nest in a safe haven.

The love birds were found breeding recently on an industrial site and the RSPB were keen to find the birds safe alternative accommodation.

Nesting

And so Fred was sent on his mission to scale the heights of the chimney and install a specially built nesting box, pictured, which the birds will hopefully come to view as their home.

The man who reunited Fred with his first chimney is Tony Johnson, Bolton's RSPB group leader.

He explained that the birds had been spotted in the Barrow Bridge area and it was highly likely that they had been prospecting the chimney as a nest.

"Fred is working on the chimney for the next couple of months so it's unlikely they will nest this year.

"But fingers crossed that they build a home in the chimney next year.

"The birds are extremely rare and so very important. Twenty years ago they were nearly wiped out by DDT poisoning." "Because they are rare it is highly important that their nesting site is safe because there are some unscrupulous people out there who would steal their eggs or their young."

● Back up to the crow's nest goes Dibnah . . . but it's not just another bird's-eye view!

A mere speck at the top of the steeple, Mr Dibnah goes to work on demolition.

THE LAST OF A LOCAL LANDMARK

STARTING at the top is sometimes the recipe for success but for Fred Dibnah it is a necessity that spells the end for St. John's Church.

The 150ft steeple, which has towered above Radcliffe New Road for more than a century, is the last major part of the church to be demolished. The main body lies in rubble already and the spire will soon follow.

The man with the best view of the situation is steeplejack Fred Dibnah. He has seen many great pieces of architecture fall but he is still sad at the loss of a building like St. John's Church. He works alone at the top throwing down the stone piece by piece.

The 28 cwt cast-steel bell is still in the spire and Mr Dibnah fears that the stones he drops through will bring it down, but the debris must be dropped on the inside because of the risk of damaging graves.

IN YOUR VIEW — AND MINE
FRED IS TV'S MOST UNLIKELY STAR

AN unlikely star emerged from your letters last week. It's surprising because he's just an ordinary bloke — and in a repeat series late on Sunday nights. But Fred Dibnah, the Bolton steeplejack, seems to have captured your imaginations.

● Reminds me of my father who travelled the home countries as a steeplejack. Unlike Mr Dibnah, he'd no other interests, but worked at this hard and dangerous job until he was 82. — Mrs J. Fraser, 15-2 Hutchison Loan, Edinburgh.

● Such a down-to-earth person for a steeplejack! I admire the way his wife gets involved in all his projects. — Mrs M. Petty, 42 Kennedy Gdns., Billingham.

● What a variety of work Fred does. He's a real jack of all trades. I look forward to the rest of this excellent series. —Freda Anderson, 14 Priory Green, Newcastle.

Fred tells me he's still climbing chimneys and playing with steam engines. He was on his way to Carnforth Railway Museum with wife Alison to look at the engines when we spoke.

He says he's had more letters than ever with the TV repeats. "A new show tacked on to this series will show a great big chimney coming down—better than the one they show every week," he says.

The Dibnah's have three daughters, Jane (14), Lorna (12) and Caroline (5).

Chimney climb to danger

POLICE had to coax down a man who diced with death by climbing 250 feet up a mill chimney last night.

The young man, who has not been named, scrambled in his stocking feet up ladders which had been fixed to Darwen's 320 feet high India Mill chimney by Bolton steeplejack Fred Dibnah.

The distressed man, who is thought to have had a domestic dispute, was persuaded by police to inch his way down the icy rungs as horrified onlookers watched.

He is being treated in hospital.

Fred had strung his chain of ladders to the top of the town's famous landmark for a charity stunt last weekend. But it had to be called off because of high winds.

Drinks topple Fred Dibnah

STEEPLEJACK and TV personality Fred Dibnah celebrated rather too well after successfully demolishing yet another chimney, Bolton magistrates were told today.

And it cost him his driving licence for 12 months when the court heard he was more than twice above the legal blood-alcohol limit when stopped by police.

Dibnah, aged 50, of Radcliffe Road, Bolton, admitted driving with an excess of alcohol in his blood. He was fined £200 and ordered to pay £25 costs. He also

By Patricia Roberts

admitted speeding and was fined £25.

Mr Peter Cave, prosecuting, said that Dibnah was spotted by a policeman on Manchester Road, Bolton, on June 23 driving a Land-Rover between 46 and 48 mph.

When he was stopped the policeman thought his breath smelt of alcohol. Tests showed he had 72 micrograms of alcohol per 100 mls of blood.

Mr Brendan Hegerty, defending, said that on the day of the

offence Dibnah had been working in Liverpool demolishing a chimney.

His was a difficult and dangerous job which put great strain on the individuals involved. It had taken many days of hard work to prepare the chimney.

The chimney was demolished without any problems and afterwards Dibnah and his team celebrated "a little too well" to release the tensions

Mr Hegerty said Dibnah had held a clean licence for many years and fully appreciated the foolishness of what had happened.

Fred Dibnah

- Fred never drank tea, preferring instead coffee or Guinness.

- Although intelligent, he was extremely poor at writing, spelling and maths - because as a child he had his mind on steam engines during lessons and hated school.

- He once allegedly received a scathing letter from a gay steam engine driver, because of his political incorrectness!

- Cruelty to children or animals would make him physically cry at times.

- His all time favourite film was 'Titanic' starring Kate Winslet.

- Apart from being in Germany with the Army at 21, he only ever left the UK once; in 1997 to film a Kellogg's Cornflakes commercial in South Africa.

- Fred had a stalker in 1996 to which he referred as *'Miss Two-Parrots'* because she kept a pair of budgies!

- He did NOT wear his cap in bed – even to sleep in!

- He had a splendid set of dentures with a gold tooth, but refused to wear them labelling them 'too flashy'

- Curiously enough, Fred is laid to rest with his FEET pointing TOWARDS his headstone!

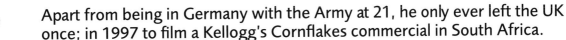

THE GREAT CANVEY ISLAND CHIMNEY DISASTER
BY FRED AND SHEILA DIBNAH

This is a story about knocking down a 450 foot high concrete chimney, 11 inches thick weighing 2,500 tons. In my opinion it was bordering on failure before I touched it!

Having never been to Canvey in my life, we set off towards Essex, as we got close I could see in the distance a lot of concrete pipes, silver pipes, cream steam, black steam, all sorts of stuff, and amongst it there's a very large chimney sticking up. I'm thinking to myself, I hope to God it's not that.

We steam onto site and are met by Rodney and his mate (from Health and Safety), these guy's looked like they had come straight from university, brand new rigger boots and shiny tin hats, Rodney says "How many tons will one of your pit props hold up?"

Well, I've got this little book "Aniarin Bevin Timber in Mining 1942" thick wartime edition, and it's got details how to make the pit props for the mining men. Apparently a piece of wood 5 inches diameter and 4 foot long will hold 50 odd tons. I told this to Rodney and his mate. They looked at me with disbelief.

The main contractor, a gentleman called Mr Skudder from London was there and he wanted to blow the arse out of it with the dynamite and have all the glory. They had built this great bandstand with a corrugated iron roof, staircases, handrails, kicking boards, fully seated and everything for the Civic Dignitaries of Canvey Island so they could sit watching the drop.

72

"...we're going to use the bottom bits, the bits that dogs pee on, where they're a lot thicker". I replied.

When the telegraph poles arrived, somebody had been buggering about with them, there were a four foot length missing out of one end. And I'm suspicious of this, so when Rodney and his mate arrived I said, "What have you been doing with my telegraph poles?" Rodney says "We did a test, it held 58 tons before it busted". "Well we're going to use the bottom bits, the bits that dogs pee on, where they're a lot thicker". I replied.

We set to work and are averaging about five foot a day with the Stihll saw 2½ inches in, a CP9 jigger pick which is the smallest demolition pick you can get. Now the secret weapon was Big Bertha, you've seen Irish men in the road with a big drill? Well it's like one of them, but adapted to work sideways.

Every day Rodney and his mate would come and have a look "Well there's no real weight on the wood yet is there Rodney?" and off they would go, these lads were really earning their brass.

Over the next few days were doing well, we're about five foot off half way on the left hand side. It doesn't do to go to the pub for your lunch too early when you're doing work of this nature. But I'd said to my wife Sheila "We'll see you at the pub at 1 o'clock."

I was getting another 5 or 6 inches out of the right hand side and it was like chiselling Weetabix. Then all of a sudden without much of a to-do and not much noise a bloody big piece flit off the side like, Christ I thought, that is excessive bloody pressure from above!

I'm stroking my chin. The other fella's gone white, and then [boom] another piece has come off. Bollocks, we're no longer in charge; it's coming on its own! Forget the tools, the hammers, the Land Rover, the lot. Run!

"Well there's no real weight on the wood yet is there Rodney?" and off they would go, these lads were really earning their brass.

73

I proposed running in the opposite direction and fell over a reinforcing bar ending up on my back looking at the most horrible vision I've ever seen in my life. The arse end's blowing out of it. How are you going to run away from something thirty five feet diameter that's coming down? And I thought it's pointless getting up and running because you might be running the wrong way! The thing to do is watch the top and see what happens, and whichever way the top starts to deviate you leg it in the opposite direction!

It came straight down for forty feet and settled. When they'd completed it in 1974, they'd put a bloody wooden lid on the top to stop the rain getting at the refractory. The air pressure had built up and blew the bloody lid straight off - and it's heading for Canvey Island town centre like a giant gramophone record! I'm thinking we're in real trouble here.

We're going to look a load of pillocks I thought we've been here for three weeks and just reduced it by 40 foot without me striking a match.

The thing to do is watch the top and see what happens, and whichever way the top starts to deviate you leg it in the opposite direction!

It came straight down for forty feet and settled. When they'd completed it in 1974, they'd put a bloody wooden lid on the top to stop the rain getting at the refractory. The air pressure had built up and blew the bloody lid straight off - and it's heading for Canvey Island town centre like a giant gramophone record! I'm thinking were in real trouble here.

It had had this nasty shock by coming straight for forty feet, but it must have still been leaning, and all the oil drums that were laid out for us to get it down the middle of. Then just like slow motion it fell straight down the bloody middle, beautiful, you know.

And now the other side of the story from Fred's widow Sheila.

"The bloody thing fell down a day early ..." said Fred about the Canvey Island Chimney disaster during his after-dinner-talks. I know – I was there. He always told the story with such eloquence, but never mentioned that he almost gave me cardiac arrest on that day with his antics!

"We'll meet you in the pub at dinnertime". He'd said to me that morning. It was almost noon, and setting off from the hotel with Nathan in the back of the car, he quipped, "Mum, I can't see Fred's chimney". Canvey Island is flat, and the steel-reinforced concrete 450ft chimney weighing almost 2,500 tons was a prominent feature on the skyline. "Nonsense," I said – but still he insisted it was not there.

"Aye, well – nobody's been killed, but it's bloody knackered up their fancy day tomorrow, like." He grinned at me, "Fell down a day early ..."

He was right. The chimney was no more. I sped off towards the demolition site, nearly mowing down an old woman pushing a shopping trolley, and got to the perimeter of the site to see a cloud of dust rising in the distance from the ground like some evil apparition. Glum-faced demolition workers, who told me the chimney had accidentally collapsed, met me at the gates. I feared the worst; I thought Fred would be dead, I knew his team of men would have been working on it when it fell.

Before I could ask about possible fatalities, a beaming Fred came sauntering over to the car looking like a naughty little boy caught out. "Aye, well – nobody's been killed, but it's bloody knackered up their fancy day tomorrow, like." He grinned at me, "Fell down a day early ..."

Fred saw the funny side, he said. However, in the pub later that night, badly shaken, he told tales about how he ran away as the job went out of control and he'd tripped over a steel reinforcing bar, only to watch the concrete giant waiver only yards away from where he lay. He and his team could have been killed. His thoughts as he ran centred on the men helping him. Had they escaped in time? It was the most fateful chimney in his thirty years career as a steeplejack, Fred addressed the gathered group, and expanding on the tale, told them he had nibbled out about six inches too much from the cut in the base of the chimney. That had caused the weight to unevenly disperse, and thus caused stress lines in the concrete, resulting in the eventual collapse.

It was always his manner to laugh things off in public. However, in private I knew how disturbed he had been by the incident. He blamed it on interference from the 'health and safety' men, undermining his confidence by carrying out tests on his wooden telegraph poles. Educated men, with new rigger boots and shiny hard hats - as he put it – were to blame for not letting him get on with a job he had successfully done since being a young man.

Fred was in shock, and it took him several months to come to terms with what had happened at Canvey Island. Nevertheless, like the tough man he was, it did not deter him from future chimney-felling jobs as we all know. Right up to six months before he sadly left us for a much higher place than a chimney, he was still knocking 'em down with gusto.

75

FRED'S CHIMNEY
BY FRED DIBNAH

"I've knocked down a fair few chimney's in me life, but really, I've not built too many," said Fred in 2000 to a reporter from the local press, who had come along to Radcliffe Road to ask about his newest creation - a 45ft high chimney stack that he had built in his back garden. He stood proudly gazing up at the creation, posing for the photographer. Scratching his chin and studying the brick built structure; he added, "The thing is, it's been eight years in the making. And I think it will probably be the last ever chimney stack built in Bolton. There's not many left now, but at one time when I were a kid, they were all over the place. I built a rather fancy chimney on me mam's house when I were about 17, but when I started me steam workshops after I were married like, I always reckoned I'd build another on a grander scale when I got time.

This bugger's been done in dribs and drabs over the years, you see. I've always been on with other stuff, but it's worth it now, because it will enable my steam boiler and all the tackle to run more efficiently. The top looks like stone, but it's not, it's concrete, and I made a mould out of some of them modern blue plastic 45 gallon oil drums cut down, and pieces of wood to give it the shape, then poured in the concrete and hoisted it up to the top with a block and tackle. I had a bit of a 'topping out' ceremony with the missus and that was filmed by the man from the BBC. Think he thought we were a bit barmy, because we had our horn gramophone up there too. Rather nice though. They did a lot of that in the old days when the steeplejacks had finished building the thing."

This bugger's been done in dribs and drabs over the years, you see

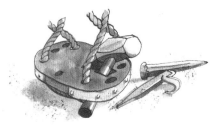

76

The House At Nob End!

By
Sheila Dibnah

Time was always at a premium for Fred. However, now and then, the urge would take him to 'go for a walk' and I would eagerly look forward to these happy, carefree days usually midweek in the height of summer.

The destination would always be the same. A walk along the canal bank at a place called Prestolee, near Kersley just outside Bolton. Close by were some old, derelict locks on the disused part of the canal. A staircase of six, sadly overgrown, dry and seemingly lost forever. It was a very ethereal and romantic place, and Fred and I would go wandering arm in arm near 'our locks' pondering the great industrial days of the busy canal, and continuing on foot along the canal path as the sun shimmered down on a local grey, stone lined reservoir. Eventually we ended up at a nice pub called 'The Horseshoe Inn' at Ringley for our lunch. After a plate of their homemade cheese and onion pie (which turned into steak and onion whenever Fred was alone) we would sit over a pint or two, reminiscing and chatting to John, the Landlord about the old days around the area.

Fred was President of the Manchester Bolton & Bury Canal Society dedicated to restoring the canal through Bolton, Bury and Salford to rejoin the national waterways, so this area held a special place in his heart.

One sunny day, we stood by the disused canal and looked upwards towards a large Victorian detached residence with massive windows and lots of land located near 'our locks'. It was perched right above the canal on a slight banking with a commanding view of the surrounding area right across the Irwell Valley at a place unusually called 'Nob End', which brought much glee and a naughty sparkle to Fred's eye, who insisted it was named after his favourite pastime!

The property was ramshackle, empty and up for sale, a couple of passing locals informed us, and so we ventured up the overgrown path to investigate further. The house itself appeared as Dickensian, austere, bleak as any local folklore ghost story of old canal men, and waif-like apparitions. I got excited as I peered in through the windows, and spotted the huge marble fireplaces and elaborate cornice mouldings in the well-sized room.

Later that day at home, we talked about it and Fred agreed we should go back and have a proper look. The next-door neighbour held a key, and we returned within two days to see if we could have a viewing indoors.

Ripe for renovation, within its solid walls it held vast potential for someone of rare ability like Fred, who by now was noticing the large well-proportioned high-ceilinged rooms, lovely door architraves and plaster mouldings. He loved the idea, and said the place could be made very beautiful with antiques, heavy drapes and traditional furnishings. A farmer called Stanley had resided in it for most of his life; sadly having died a few months ago aged 80, and so the place was now up for grabs at a bargain price of £160,000. Although a bit run-down it was pure magic, and if ever a place was perfect to turn into a steam heritage centre, this was it. Fred totally agreed as we trudged around the perimeter inspecting the grounds, finding an old Anderson shelter around the back of the property, which set Fred off on one of his famous monologues.

You could imagine this headland: traction engines, pit-head gear and gas lamps on some damp foggy evening catapulting you back in time to when smog and soot hung in the air and over the canal like a thick, sulphur smelling blanket before the 'modern world' came along with it's 'clean air act'. We imagined present-day curious locals, taking in our unique industrial views upon the hillside during crisp, stark days of winter, before visitors eventually arrived in springtime to see the steam paraphernalia in action. We would proudly call it 'The Dibnah Experience of Steam'.

We talked incessantly during the following days about cobbled driveways, pithead gears, belts, wheels, pulleys, old-fashioned tearooms. For a while, my hope that we might eventually move there seemed a distinct possibility and we were ready to make an offer.

However, I woke one morning three weeks later, my hopes dashed. Fred was becoming increasingly vague about it, and avoided the subject, stalling, saying he did not think we could afford it, or someone else might buy it first. It was an excuse.

Looking around seeing how much of Fred's spirit was held within the walls where we currently lived at 121 Radcliffe Road, the place he had restored during his 30 years of living there, I suddenly realised I was way off beam if I ever thought he would give this up. I could never really expect Fred to leave here, it was his entire world and realistically I knew he never would. He loved his back yard.

We had talked previously about how we would recruit volunteers to move his steam workshops, but it simply was not going to happen once I stopped to think about the implications and instinctively knew that he would never really agree to the move. It was a pipe dream. Not only that: the warning signs had been peppered throughout his entire earlier conversations as we excitedly made our plans for the other place. "If I were forty years younger, cock, we could do this/do that with it ..." I now realised how he felt and when I finally broached the subject over breakfast one day, he looked a bit relieved that I had spoken up.

So we never got to live near 'Our Locks', but would occasionally return to see progress on the house in the hands of someone else. In a rare moment of candour in the hospice after he became seriously ill, he whispered to me one day, *"You know cock, if I'd have been a younger man, I would have bought you that bloody house at Nob End ... it was perfect an' all ... I loved it".*

WHAT'S IT LIKE TO BE FAMOUS FRED?

ANSWERED BY FRED DIBNAH

I reckon the only thing that's ever changed about me nowadays, is the size of the bloody crowd when I'm telling me stories on a steam rally or in a pub!

Fame has never altered me; I've always been the same since being a very young man. When you see them blokes on telly, with their fancy ways and funny clothes, I think, "What the hell have you ever done to be famous for?" I was never any good at telling jokes, and I didn't think it was all that important anyway. Me mam wanted me to play the piano, and me dad was a good dancer, like our kid. I wanted to be like the men up in the sky who were like gods to me when I was a small boy, and I was lucky enough to end up making my living from being like them mending factory chimneys.

One of my earliest memories weren't about a factory chimney, but a domestic one! There were a neighbour in the next-but-one street called Mr Tranter, a bit posher than we were because their house had leaded windows, and they were always having their front door painted with them funny patterns done with a heart-grainer to resemble wood like they used to do back then.

One day, I noticed a bit of a commotion outside their house, and I went over to see what the matter was. Mr Tranter told me their cat, Blackie, had gotten stuck up the parlour chimney or summat. I went in to see if I could do owt, but the bloody thing started hissing and spitting at me when I eventually shoved a brush steel up the chimney to try and dislodge the creature. It's a bit like that time later on in me life when I were mending a factory chimney and a cat got stuck up there one day after going up the ladder, and I had to try and rescue it.

Anyway, this bloody cat of Mr Tranter's wouldn't come down, and then suddenly – whoosh! A great cloud of black soot all over Mrs Tranter's posh hearthrug and I remember thinking I bet the poor bugger would be more terrified of his wife's reaction to that happening when she came back from the shops than the damned cat being wedged up the chimney.

Anyway, after I'd been on telly, the BBC and ITV were there pointing their cameras skywards up at me when I rescued the cat from the top of a factory chimney. The cat, a red one, which after it had been up the chimney all night was a black one the following morning, ended up being on all the local news items, and I got letters from cat lovers from all over the place. Funny thing this fame, I can tell you tales like that, but if you ask me where I was doing one of me after dinner talks last week, I couldn't tell you. I'm not that bothered about being famous.

Hell, before the telly came along, I never ventured far away from home. I'd lie awake in my bed some nights thinking, 'If I had a few grand in the bank, I could finish me engine, and not bother about money so much.' But you've gotta get on in this life, and it's an ill wind that blows no bugger any good. So to be honest, I don't mind it so much when people come down to my yard to see me from all over the country. I mean, it's alright because some of 'em bring me interesting stuff for me garden without me havin' to part with any green notes, so it's not that bad being famous.

MY TIME WITH FRED
A MUCH MISSED PAL!

BY
NEIL CARNEY
FRED'S RIGHT HAND MAN

I followed my father into mechanical engineering serving an apprenticeship as a fitter/turner in Liverpool. I joined the Lancashire Traction Engine club in 1965 when it was quite new.

I first met Fred Dibnah at one of the early traction engine rally's at Burtonwood in the late 1960s. He had just bought his Steam Roller and had embarked on the long task of completely rebuilding it. This included a new boiler which he made himself. Fred had consulted retired boiler makers and acquired all the necessary tools, many of which were available from these knowledgeable men. He must have been an ideal student for these men, because with Fred it was once shown, never forgotten, and because of this he soon acquired all the skills to do the job.

The construction of a boiler has to be inspected at regular stages so the workmanship has to be of the highest standard. Fred's was a riveted construction; he never became a welder- no certificates for our Fred!

I kept in touch with Fred during the rebuild, but did not actually play any part in it. He worked under a tarpaulin slung between the trees in his back garden in the early days. He did eventually build a substantial shed which grew over the years to become the "Victorian Factory" that we know today.

I took early retirement in 1989 and Fred got to hear of this. He was without a mate at that time and was overhauling a steam engine for Gwynedd Council. They intended to put the engine back into use as an attraction at a craft centre they were developing at Parc Glynllifon South Carnarvon. Fred asked me if I would help him build the engine, this was a job that suited me fine, as we were to work Monday to Friday in Wales for about three months. We finally left the engine in working order, driven by a boiler donated by a local bakery, which we installed.

I continued with Fred on the steeple jacking side of his work, during a five year period, 1989-1994 our time together was more or less divided between steeple jacking and "playing in't garden" as he would put it. This involved working on any of his fourteen machines, all driven from his steam driven line shafting. His beautiful little yard engine called Caroline started it's life driving a mechanical stoker at an old mill – it was made in Bolton!

My involvement with the chimney work consisted of pulling the ladders and decking up to his working level, and supplying any materials or equipment Fred required. I had a lot of free time down below, but I had to be ready if anything was needed upstairs.

It was my job to paint the guttering and downspouts on a small church while Fred pointed the steeple up above me. I was particlly proud that I managed to modify the clock at the same church as it was becoming troublesome. Much to the delight of the Vicar.

I assisted on about 15 chimney drops during my five happy years with Fred. My job was the"gardening" which involved keeping the working area clean and tidy by removing the bricks which were cut from the chimney base. I also cut the props [usually telegraph poles] to the exact length. Fred always invited me to do this with his chainsaw and he reckoned I got them more square at the cut than he could, "it's these glasses" he would say when he cut one himself and found it "a bit out".

When I attended the dropping, I was usually required to drive the Landrover and compressor back home to Radcliffe Road - I am not a drinking man myself, but would leave Fred to take the glory for a job well done.

I assisted on about 15 chimney drops during my five happy years with Fred. My job was the"gardening" which involved keeping the working area clean and tidy

85

The only chimney drop that went wrong during my time was due to Fred's explanation of how the job was done, in the pub, on the night before. This was at Cockermouth, in Cumbria. Some members of his audience did the job overnight… but failed. All the props were burned away, but miraculously the chimney had stood its ground. At about 5 o'clock in the morning on the day of the drop the police called on us to tell us the tale. Fred and I attended the scene straight away, and managed to put in a few new props. The reason the chimney had not fallen was simply that the "slot" was not fully cut half way. This is a job that is always left until the morning of the drop.

The local Fire Brigade had been called but they would not go near it. The Commander had decided that with there being no danger to life and limb or any property in the vicinity and the site was obviously clear that they would take no risks. It did fall, later in the day under Fred's full control. When "our own fire" was lit.

Another strange thing occurred at Whitworth. It was a straightforward job, but when the fire was lit, there appeared to be a strong downdraught in the chimney which caused the fire to burn outside up the brickwork instead of burning through the props. Nothing could be done but hope for a gust of wind in the right direction to turn the flames inside. After about ten anxious minutes all went well and the chimney duly fell, exactly on line, but a little late!

After leaving Fred in 1994, I kept in touch with him to follow the progress with his Aveling Steam Tractor- the one used on his last tour with the BBC. I had but little interest in his mine shaft and I sincerely hoped that it would not take too much of his time off completing his tractor. It would have been a tragedy had he not completed it in time for his tour. However Fred made it, and I am sure that his desire to complete 27 years work extended his life by some two years.

I lost a good friend in Fred, we did not share social time together, but the five years we "worked", if you can call "playing int garden" work, were most enjoyable. He appreciated my engineering background and I certainly appreciated his practical approach to a problem. Nothing ever got the better of Fred, apart from calculation; he tended to leave that to me, but had I not been there he would have found some other way of getting a tricky job done.

Fred's MBE was never awarded to a more fitting person; his interests lay in a time when we had an Empire! I don't doubt that, right now, he will be discussing his "methods" with his mentor, Mr I K Brunell.

I was honoured that Fred had requested that I drove his Steam Roller Betsy on the day of his funeral. It was a duty that I carried out with precision, respect, and sadness. Rest in peace Fred.

Neil Carney

The people we met on the way, and the warmness of them, was a true highlight. The engine was special to me as well...

But he was serious about work. The work we did with him on various projects was always carried out in the old fashioned way. Even if it was easier and quicker to do it the modern way, he wouldn't have any of it.

I went with Fred to his last but one chimney drop at Brandlesholme, near Bury. It was funny really, because he asked me to go with him when he was sorting out the contract part. I said I didn't know 'owt about dropping chimney's but he goes "Naah, mate – you look the part!" So I kept nodding and smiling while he talked to the gaffer. When he'd got the job, I went with him on the first day, and worked alongside him for a couple of hours, but I hurt my knee, so that were that – I couldn't go again!

I've always said though, one of the greatest things about meeting Fred was that trip where we went round Britain on the engine. The people we met on the way, and the warmness of them, was a true highlight. The engine was special to me as well, because I gave him a lift with building it, I was involved in a bit of everything. I'm not an engineer, but I did some labouring for Fred, it was more or less assembling everything, really. Various parts hadn't been made such as the throat plate. When he had a new one made, it was x-rayed and found to have cracks in, so we had to have another one done. That held us up a bit. The biggest job I did was the stays which were done by hammer; he wouldn't have them done by rivet gun.

The biggest job I did was the stays which were done by hammer; he wouldn't have them done by rivet gun.

All knocked over, the threaded stays, inside and out, by hand. He's asked me if I were any good at it you see, and I told him I'd never done any, so he showed me, like, and did one himself, and I told him I could manage that. It was a noisy job though, many thousands of hammer blows, especially the inside ones - you come out and you are deaf! Took me many weeks, but he was happy with what I had done.

I can't remember the exact date when he told me he'd got cancer; I had only known him a spell before that. He just wanted to carry on basically; they'd given him about twelve months. Fred just said to me one day "We are doing this series, like, and you are coming!" I told him my wife Wendy might not be keen on being on her own at night, but Fred didn't take any notice. We were right on the last minute because of working on the mineshaft, but we completed the engine in time for this epic journey.

The director would say "we'll not be filming on Monday, Fred's not so good but come down to the yard just in case". Then Fred would appear, fit as a fiddle, and say "Are we ready for off then, or what". Just like that. He wanted to press on there were no stopping him, he was determined. It happened more than once. He was very ill by then, but was still as friendly with everybody.

The engine became his passion, and the wonderful trip we did spurred him on. My job was steersman, I'd had no experience, but I did all right I suppose, especially once the steering chains were shortened, made the job a lot easier. I remember coming down Llanberris Pass, a beautiful location, my favourite as well was around the Peak District, those long drives.

It was something Fred had always wanted to do, drive around the country on his engine and I was honoured to be a part of it. We had a few teething troubles at first, but they got sorted out. Anyway, end of the day, there was no real problems and it was the experience of a lifetime for us both.

The director would say "we'll not be filming on Monday, Fred's not so good" but come down to the yard just in case.

89

My name is Alf Molyneux. And I, like many others, have been touched by the spell of Fred Dibnah. In fact it may seem hard to believe, but I had never even seen him on telly before we met, and I never had any interest in steam. All that changed when I was fortunate enough to be introduced to Fred through a friend, while out drinking at a local club.

This is my story of my short time with my great pal, the late Fred Dibnah MBE.

I've worked in the mining industry most of my life, and of course, when Fred and I got chatting in the club, Fred got excited about this and invited me down to see his pit head gear in the yard. While I was doing the grand tour of the place, which took about an hour with him telling me where stuff came from, he says "Can you give us a lift for a bit, mate?" So I did, and that's how it all started, me coming down to the yard from then on.

Eventually, a group of my mates started coming down as well. These were men interested in mining. One Saturday, I'd mentioned that I was going to Fred's yard, and told them about his pit head gear. They all wanted to see it, and so Saturdays became a regular day for us all to go to Fred's and help out wherever we could. Saturday's at the yard became like open house, and people would wander in to meet him. Fred had time for them all.

My mate Jimmy Crooks and I got a big team together, so we could get stuck in sinking the pit shaft and other jobs that Fred was on with. He wanted to get his mine up and running, it would have been an authentic replica, actually passing through a coal seam, because the yard is in a mining area, but the idea wasn't to mine coal really, just look as though we were. It would have happened too, but for him passing on. It was his dream to own his own pit.

They were good, enjoyable times because he was a nice sociable chap and I recall when I first met him some blokes wanting an autograph and Fred spoke to them like he'd known them all his life. That's how he was, you see, right friendly, like. I never knew him to refuse an autograph, photograph or chance of a chat, he'd talk to anyone.

Ian was Fred's helper around the yard. It was his job to get steam up for the workshop and keeping the boiler stoked. He played a big part in helping Fred to complete his Aveling tractor.

Ian was also Fred's "Chief Engine Polisher" and used to say "There's no-one in England that can polish an engine as good as yon mon".

91

THE WORST DAY
OF OUR LIVES
BY
SHEILA DIBNAH

It was awful. Sheer bloody awful. The consultant sat in front of us and said, "Well, Mr Dibnah, I'm afraid there's no easy way to tell you, but you've got twelve months left to live if we cannot arrest the disease".

What do you say to that? What can anyone say? Fred had already undergone one cycle of chemotherapy. It had initially worked, we were elated - but now this ...the cancer had returned and the consultant's words hit us like lightening. It was official, they did not think that they could cure it this time; however, they were going to try some new stuff from America which had been shown to be effective in curing cancers similar to Fred's. Another cycle of chemotherapy might just give us some hope. Hope was all we had left.

"What are you going to do?" I asked, not expecting any sort of positive answer. "I'm going to finish me engine off, cock," he firmly replied,

Cancer. That awful word. What idiot was it that once said 'sticks and stones may break my bones, but words can never hurt me'?

From that day on, Fred was determined to beat the terrible scourge of humanity. He was a true fighter. "What are you going to do?" I asked, not expecting any sort of positive answer. "I'm going to finish me engine off, cock," he firmly replied, the shock not having yet set in, "And me pit. I want to finish me pit as well". The engine in question, still in oily bits, being his Aveling & Porter Colonial Steam Tractor - which he would periodically work on. In his own words, for twenty-two years and two divorces; the pit was his dream of creating a working mock mineshaft in our back garden. Already, several years earlier he had erected the wooden pithead gear. Now his team of helpers would begin to dig a mineshaft that would later be the subject of one of his television programmes 'Dig with Dibnah'.

94

Alf Molyneux came down to help on the engine, Fred spat out the bad news. Poor Alf, he had not known Fred that long, but they'd become firm pals...

Such a shock to hear the word 'cancer' and 'returned' mentioned in the same sentence about someone you love. We went home from the hospital and drank a full bottle of wine each, and Fred said, "Naaah, I told you it would come back; I never thought it would go away". Next day, I looked at the diary in my office, it was full of speaking engagements, personal appearance and theatre dates. Fred was now at the very peak of his career as a celebrity, with all that entailed. Life for Fred had rumbled by after many years of heavy toil as a steeplejack, but now - bills were paid, luxuries had, and money not a problem. It did not matter anymore. Nothing did, except dealing with what was around the corner. Life was suddenly topsy-turvy, it made you realise that nothing in life apart from your health is very important. We made plans to return to Christies Hospital in Manchester several days later, where Fred would receive the new American drugs. The wine took effect, and temporarily dulled the inner fears, but still we both did not sleep much that night.

The next day went by in sort of a dull fog. Fred soldiered on seemingly oblivious to the bombshell that had just landed amidst his self-made world of an industrial landscape in the back yard, which constituted the very core of his soul. Alf Molyneux came down to help on the engine, Fred spat out the bad news. Poor Alf, he had not known Fred that long, but they'd become firm pals, and Alf, like Fred was a man not afraid of hard work. He was tough, having spent most of his working life as a miner. But he shed real tears that day.

I watched the activity in the garden. No different on the face of it. Work on the half-restored traction engine continued as more helpers came down; and as normal, steam rose to 100psi in the Danks boiler enabling the small engine 'Caroline' to run the workshops. A false sense of security ensued, and the distinct possibility that the wrong diagnosis had been made fleetingly crossed my mind. How could this man - so vital, still full of energy, knowledgeable and larger than life now have just less than twelve months left to live? Not fair, no justice - Fred was supposed to be invincible, wasn't he? It certainly seemed that way at times.

That very same day several months ago when we actually learned Fred had cancer was an ongoing living nightmare too, and it would never go away – even if the cancer should miraculously now be cured by an act of God, we would still remember that day.

The morning of 29th October 2000 is a day I shall never forget as long as I live. Fred had previously been poorly for some time with kidney troubles, and after having the right one removed, we thought that was the end of it. Until two chilling telephone calls changed our lives for good.

I was pottering about doing stuff in the kitchen, with Fred reading at the table close by, when the shrill ring of the old--fashioned telephone commanded attention. Fred got up, and I half-listened to the conversation. "Aye, well, we'll come up then. Why can't you tell me now, eh? Aye, alright then, this afternoon at 1pm." Fred came back after the uncharacteristically short call. Usually he was on for ages, the other person hardly getting a word in, but now he was still. Apparently, we were summoned to the hospital this afternoon to see Miss Mobb, the Consultant Urologist who had performed Fred's operation to remove the kidney.

The news was awful. The removed kidney contained a malignant tumour, and Fred would need a series of chemotherapy to remove any remaining cancerous cells. This would start within the next week, and strange drugs were mentioned with alien sounding names that seemed to suggest something more akin to poisonous substances rather than life saving therapy at a cellular level. I started to cry, feeling lost and helpless; Fred sat there and asked a few direct questions. "Will this bugger kill me, or can you fettle it?" Faced with such candour, Miss Mobb said she did not know for certain, but tests showed the cancer had not spread into the fatty tissue, which therefore suggested removal of the kidney might have isolated the spread of the disease, but he would receive chemotherapy to be on the safe side.

The morning of 29th October 2000 is a day I shall never forget as long as I live. Fred had previously been poorly for some time with kidney troubles

Advised to go home for an hour or two to mull things over, we were instructed to return to the hospital at 3pm to speak to a cancer specialist, Dr Wylie, who was coming over from Christies Hospital in Manchester that afternoon. Then, with a plan of action decided upon, we would know more about the type of cancer Fred had developed, and his chances of beating it.

We left the hospital in a stupor, and returned home to Radcliffe Road. Opening the door on arrival, the telephone was ringing. A flash of annoyance keenly stabbed at my worried mind. "For chrissake, we can't even have bad news in peace!" I spat out "don't answer the bloody thing!" However, Fred suggested it might be the hospital. It was indeed from the hospital, but not the consultant, a more familiar voice spoke out: "Sheila, your dad has had an accident, he's in the hospital and I'm here with him" It seemed like he was injured but my mum did not say how or why, just insisted I came up straight away.

We left the hospital in a stupor, and returned home to Radcliffe Road. Opening the door on arrival, the telephone was ringing.

Immediately, we set off back to the hospital, the nightmare never ending, eventually entering into the A&E annex to find my mum, tear-stained and shaking, being comforted by a doctor in a white coat. The story unfolded: my parents had recently had some work done on their semi on the outskirts of Bolton by a band of property dodgers or 'cowboys' and these lowlifes had left a mess behind after being paid in cash. My dad, aged 72 and a proud man, humiliated by the experience had decided to go up a ladder to check the guttering on the roof left in a shoddy state by the bogus workers. The ladders had slipped and he had crashed to the ground 21ft below, bashing his brains out on the stone flags. The hospital said there was nothing more they could do for him, he was on life support, but technically brain dead.

We entered the room, and my dad lay on the gurney with his misshapen head clearly visible under the extensive, pink-stained bandages. He was near to death, with extensive damage to the brain. Tubes, monitors and equipment surrounded his pale half-naked body. A nurse enquiring if Fred still wanted to see Dr Wylie, the specialist from Christie's hospital, eventually interrupted the 'bleep-bleep-bleep' of the machines and distracted me from the flickering green line of the monitor. I nodded my head to say he should go. The machine ticked by the last few seconds of my dad's life and someone switched off the life support. I held his cool hand as he died. My mum sat there in shock, staring with disbelief.

humiliated by the experience had decided to go up a ladder to check the guttering on the roof left in a shoddy state by the bogus workers.

After what seemed like two hours travelling on hell's train of cataclysmic events, Fred wearily returned to the waiting area to ask if my mum and I were all right, and muttered something about coffee. All three of us left the room, and I cannot honestly tell you what happened next - although I do recall Fred saying something about Dr Wylie telling him that he was suffering from the most aggressive form of cancer there was, and the chances of curing it were minimal.

Each of us now trapped in our own private hell, it was really the beginning of the end at that moment in time, for not only our marriage, which gradually became derailed and is another longer story, but also Fred's very existence. We needed each other to be strong, but how could we be after this? This was the worst moment in my entire life, and so too was it Fred's. Both for different reasons. Life would never be the same again.

So today, after several months grieving for my dad, I looked out through the window and watched Fred sprightly run towards Alf with a white-hot rivet held in a pair of tongs, and saw the determination on his face. I knew he would finish that engine.

Despite two gruelling cycles of chemotherapy, pain and the single-minded conviction he wanted to do a final BBC 2 series called 'Made in Britain' with friend and producer David Hall, I knew Fred would live each remaining day in the same manner he had always tackled his life up to then; with brio, hard work, skill and the sheer tenacity to succeed at anything he put his mind to.

The cancer did not go away with the second cycle of chemotherapy. Fred later refused to participate in trials for some new, so-called wonder drug not yet tested on humans; labelling it 'his Joseph Mengle treatment' (after the Nazi doctor who experimented on Jews in the Second World War), the quality of life was all that mattered to him now. He did beat the cancer in a way, he won the battle if not the war, living on two years longer than expected. During those two final years, he brought to life the engine he so wanted to complete before he died, and undeterred, had the chance to drive it around the country under its own head of steam and receive an M.B.E for his services to television and broadcasting.

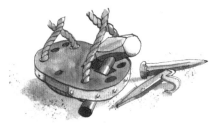

A DATE WITH HER MAJESTY

BY
SHEILA DIBNAH

The Beatles were number one, the summer hot, and I was just seven growing up in sixties Bolton. The Queen was coming to town, and we traipsed off at playtime to see her pass by the end of the road. I often wonder nowadays if Fred had heard she was coming to town that day. Being a bit of a Royalist, maybe he too was in the crowd. On the other hand, perhaps he would be stuck up a ladder mending a chimney somewhere in his hometown? In any case, it would be over forty years before fate would assemble us all under one roof. A particularly fine roof too – Buckingham Palace.

We set off for London on a warm early July day in 2004. Months previously, we had received several letters from the Palace, the first one prompted a response from Fred: "Some bugger's 'avin me on. Who'd give a bloody gong to a daft pillock like me?" It nearly went unanswered. He held a cup of coffee, shaking his head in wonder at the picture of the Queen and Prince Phillip in his engine shed, and repeated the sentiment. It was only when I replied and we got a firm date arranged did he take the matter seriously.

Now here it was, the 7th day of July and we were in the hotel room at the side of Buckingham Palace ready to meet Her Royal Highness. We had travelled down the previous day from Bolton, and I was brushing his jacket as Fred dressed for the most important occasion of his life - it was the first time I had seen him nervous, but he was still cracking jokes. "Should of come down with me bloody Roller cock, if Her Majesty could have thrown me a few bags of coal on, I could have flattened the gravel by Royal Appointment. Can you imagine the steam men if I had a royal crest on the side that said "Fred Dibnah by Royal Appointment". that would get um talking eh?

I had hired for him a lovely dark morning suit and cream waistcoat and cravat, set off with a fine top hat. He studied and fiddled with the outfit, particularly the trousers. "Who the bloody hell designs these daft things, eh? There's no belt loop, how can you keep the buggers up?" I showed him the adjustable waistband. "What the hell good is that with the size of my beer belly, I'll end up exposing me wedding tackle to the Queen of England if I'm not careful ...!

He also moaned about not being able to keep the top hat straight on his head, and stuffed it with yesterday's evening news, immediately solving the problem, but the trousers presented a bit more of a dilemma. He had an idea, and explained later... "Aye, well, some time ago – I'd made me own braces in me shed out of some dog-clips and bits of old string. I don't like them modern ones they make these days, no good when you are doing 'owt a bit strenuous, like. The old ones were better in the days when you had buttons on your trousers, but you can't get them now, it's like owt else, but these home-made braces do the trick. You just hook 'em through your belt loops.

Anyway, this particular morning standing there getting ready to meet the Queen, there were 'nowt else for it but use the ones I'd made. So I punched bloody great holes in these posh pants with a fork we'd knicked from the hotel, and shoved the dog clips through. The missus weren't too keen on me going to meet the Queen of England with me pants held up with string...but it worked all right. Anyway, no bugger knew, so I don't know what she were on about!"

We left the hotel and walked to the palace gates with Jack and Roger. David Hall was there preserving the occasion with his film crew and we stopped and spoke for a while. It was blowing a gale, and Fred held on to his top hat while my floaty dress whipped around my legs. Soon it was time to go through the gates, and walk over the gravelled forecourt towards the famous building. Entering the palace, we were met by a polite, well-groomed usher, who told us to proceed up a massive, rather ornate Rococco-style gold staircase. A magical feeling ensued as we noticed the old masters lining the walls. This was it – inside the palace! At the top of the stairs, Fred was instructed to go into a side room, while the boys and I were escorted into the elaborate Ballroom used for state functions.

Aband located high on a decorative balcony played old standards as we waited, looking around the room taking in the sea of colourful hats and posh frocks as Fred would call them.

Eventually, we stood as the Queen, resplendent in a lime green outfit with a huge diamond broach entered to our left. She was accompanied by liveried guards and proceeded to the front of the ballroom. A long table covered in thick damask carried the awards placed on small plump cushions, and the Queen stood in front of this.

Soon, a fanfare of trumpets blared and the ceremony began. We watched as worthy people from all walks of life received Knighthoods, OBEs and MBEs. Then it was Fred's turn. "Doctor Frederick Dibnah for services to television and broadcasting..." the cut-glass voice of the announcer said over the public address system. Fred entered the room, and briefly bowed in front of the Queen. A short exchange took place, and I saw Fred lean forward and cup his hand to his good ear. I can just imagine it "Yer wot, cock – you'll have to speak up a bit, I'm DEAF!" The Queen pinned the medal on Fred; he bowed again and left the room.

The ceremony continued for about two hours, and finally we rose to the National Anthem as the Queen left the room. I noticed her piercing blue eyes as she looked directly at us.

Later, I asked, "What did she say to you then, Fred?" The Queen, it seems, after intimating that she always watched and liked his programmes, had said, "Are you still knocking down factory chimneys, Mr Dibnah?" And he had replied, "Yeah yer Majesty, I've got a big mortgage to pay, so I can't give up just yet – and besides, I like it!" She smiled and shook his hand after the brief exchange.

Obviously, it was a great honour meeting the Queen, and Fred was chuffed to bits that she loved all his programmes.

Obviously, it was a great honour meeting the Queen, and Fred was chuffed to bits that she loved all his programmes. However, the most heart-warming part was that as a working class man, he had made it to the palace all the way from his humble background, something that would have made his mother proud, and revealed in his comments later. _"I wish me mam could have seen it, she'd have been reet proud of me. She always wanted me to have an office job when I was younger; I wish she'd seen her Freddie in London. She'd have told all her mates down at the gasworks where she worked ... she'd have been reet proud an' all."_

Deuce

Two greats. Fred Dibnah MBE and Tennis star Tim Henman OBE.
Enjoying their medals at Buckingham Palace

6TH NOVEMBER 2004
DR. FRED DIBNAH DIES

TV personality and steeplejack Fred Dibnah, 66, has lost his three-year fight against cancer only weeks after filming his final television series.

Bolton-born Mr Dibnah, who became an unlikely celebrity, spurned treatment to tour the UK on a traction engine as part of a 12-part Television series.

Fred Dibnah cancelled all appearances and engagements in September after he was taken ill during filming the BBC series "Made in Britain".

He died on Saturday surrounded by friends and family at Bolton Hospice.

The star of over 20 documentaries leaves, Widow Sheila, brother Graham, Step-son Nathan, Daughters Jayne, Lorna and Caroline. Sons Jack & Roger.

FRED'S FUNERAL

A BIG DAY IN BOLTON BY PAUL DONOGHUE

I kept looking on the internet at the Bolton Evening News site. Fred had died on 6th November 2004 and I wanted to go to the funeral. A few weeks before I had driven to Manchester on business, once I had had my meeting I got back in the car and drove over to Bolton, I had decided to go to the Hospice and see Fred. I parked outside next to the trees, looking at the building. I then decided that Fred would be surrounded by close family, and perhaps this wasn't such a good idea. I then drove to Radcliffe Road and stood there looking through the railings at the marvellous sight before me, memories of some great times came back to me, but I cannot describe the sadness in my heart.

The funeral date was announced, it was to be on 16th November 2004 it was to be a public event with everyone invited. I took my black suit to the dry cleaners, I was going.

...it was chucking it down. I had to turn my car round a couple of miles into the journey and go back home for a coat.

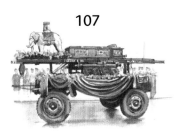

On the morning of 16th November I set off for Fred's funeral at 5.30 am. The weather was appalling, it was chucking it down. I had to turn my car round a couple of miles into the journey and go back home for a coat. It was then that I picked up my camera case and put all my equipment in the car. Then I hit the road again, with my wind screen wipers at full pelt all the way.

I could see a lot of activity in the steam sheds. As I looked around I could not believe the number of people who were gathering, women children steam men and friends.

I made good time and turned into Radcliffe Road at 7am, there were low loaders, steam men and 4 Traction engines being fettled and polished. The rain just never stopped. It was then that I saw Roy Pinches running around with his new Sony digital video camera. He scurried over to me and gave me a big handshake for a man of his size. He said "I knew you would be here, this is going to be massive, and just about everyone in Lancashire is going to be here ". We chatted for 10 minutes and then I left Roy and went to take in the scene. I looked at the bunches of flowers hanging on the railings and read the little notes of sadness. I could see a lot of activity in the steam sheds. As I looked around I could not believe the number of people who were gathering, women children steam men and friends. It was then that I decided to get my camera out and preserve what was fast becoming a film worthy and historical occasion.

I was taken aback by the attention to detail on the trailer that had been especially constructed to carry Fred's coffin. I was impressed that all the tools of a steeplejack were incorporated into the design, ropes, ladders, and pulley's, bosons chair, chisels and hammers etc. I could see the rollers that had been attached to Fred's ladders so that his coffin would easily slide on and off the trailer. I found out later that the trailer had been designed by long term friend of Fred's Michael Webber and that Michael had driven the trailer to Bolton all the way from Worthing on the south coast.

I kept looking down into the yard; there was smoke and steam bellowing out of the doors. I could see Neil Carney and Fred's youngest son Roger getting Fred's roller Betsy ready, on the other side of the shed Michael Webber and Jack Dibnah were preparing the newly completed Aveling and Porter tractor.

The rain was still pouring down, but I honestly don't think the rain was spoiling anything. What gripped you was the crowd, probably 200 people had gathered outside the house, but apart from the hissing of steam engines you could have heard a pin drop.

Suddenly everything went up a gear, the police arrived on motorbikes, and the band of 103 Regiment of the Royal Artillery Bolton Volunteers took up position at the end of Radcliffe Road. The band was going to lead the cortege. Traction engines were making their way down the road ready to take up there position in the procession. Fred's Land rover suddenly appeared through the gates. It was pushed on to the road. The Lanny was in a bit of a state and had seen much better days. It was covered in leaves and looked terrible, but someone had made the last minute decision that the Land rover should be included in the proceedings. 5 minutes later, and after some very quick hosing and cleaning the Land rover was brought up to scratch and ready to take its rightful place at the rear of Fred's living van, attached with an A frame.

The first Engine to come up the drive was Fred's trusty roller Betsy, driven by Neil Carney. As the engine pulled onto the road an immaculate black Rolls Royce hearse moved silently next to Michael Webbers trailer. As I looked around I noticed that 10 to 15 news crews had arrived to cover the funeral for local and national television, plus many press photographers.

Fred's coffin was gently pulled from the Rolls Royce hearse and then lifted slowly and carefully onto the trailer that was to carry his body around Bolton. The special rollers that had been built in to the ladders and the securing mechanism all worked perfect and Fred was now high above everyone and ready to be paraded one last time in the limelight, in his specially requested Victorian-style-funeral with steam.

While Fred was being placed on the trailer, Jack Dibnah and Michael Webber made their way slowly up the drive with the beautiful Aveling tractor. They delicately drove the engine to the front of the trailer and hooked the trailer to the rear of the engine. A look of sadness on Jack and Michael's faces told the whole story.

Fred's Land rover suddenly appeared through the gates. It was pushed on to the road. The Lanny was in a bit of a state...

Everything was almost ready; the police were talking on their radios. The engines were blowing off steam. John Howarth (funeral director) then knocked on the front door and told Fred's widow Sheila that everyone was ready. As Sheila came out of the house she acknowledged the huge crowd of onlookers, and then climbed sombrely into a beautiful white vintage Rolls Royce, supported by her son Nathan and her mother Mavis.

A few minutes later the eerie silence was broken by the deafening sound of Betsy's whistle, indicating the start of the procession. I checked my watch, it was exactly 11.15 am. The Band started playing sombre music that was fitting for the occasion. Walking up front, was the immaculately dressed John Howarth (funeral director) who took his role seriously throughout the day. By this time hundreds more people had lined the streets near to Fred's home, all wanting to pay their respects to a much loved steeplejack and television personality.

As the cortège turned onto Bradford Street and slowly over the St Peters Way Bypass, I will always remember seeing cars stopping on the carriageway and hooting their horns as they spotted Fred's funeral from below. The streets were lined 5 deep. Grannies, Granddads, Mothers, Dads, Daughters and Sons and toddlers were all stood there with their umbrellas watching this once in a lifetime happening. I saw a full class of infants with their teacher. The teacher was telling the children that Fred Dibnah was a very special man, and to wave as the engines drove past.

As I filmed, it was almost like I was on auto pilot. I had been to Bolton many times, but I had never been in Bolton town centre before, but I seemed to instinctively know where the funeral was going and where to point my camera.

As the engines pulled up outside Bolton Parish Church they were greeted by loud applause from the 1000s of people watching. It is a sight I will never forget. Not since the funeral of Princess Diana, had I witnessed such scenes.

Fred was carefully lowered from the purpose built trailer and slowly taken up the steps and along stone pathway to the church. He was followed by his Widow Sheila and other members of the family. The church was out of bounds to me, so as Fred's service took place I busied myself conducting interviews with the people outside. I heard later that it had been a lovely service and a fitting tribute to our Fred. I did see hundreds of people writing messages of condolence in the entrance to the church.

After a service taking just over an hour, the coffin came back into view, the applause started again as Fred was carefully lifted back onto the trailer for his final journey to Tonge cemetery.

...and as the cortège got closer the applause and whistles from the crowd got louder and louder. I could hear people shouting, "God bless you Fred"

Another deafening whistle from Betsy signalled that everyone was ready. A huge plume of smoke and steam engulfed the square outside the church as the engines slackened their brakes and regulators were slowly pushed forward.

The band had completed their duty and dispersed; it was now Betsy that would lead the way. I took up a vantage spot 200 yards away, and as the cortège got closer the applause and whistles from the crowd got louder and louder. I could hear people shouting, "God bless you Fred" "Rest in Peace Fred" people were truly mourning the loss of a great character.

Everyone involved in the funeral (who I have spoken to) has mentioned when the cortège went past Bolton fire station. I had to stop filming because I was trapped by the crowds. But the story goes that all the firemen and women on duty that day were stood outside the fire station in the pouring rain at the side of their appliances in full dress uniform, saluting Fred's coffin as the funeral drove past. I am grateful to David Jack who seems to have been the only person there with a camera to capture a remarkable photo.

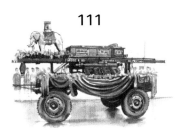

While the funeral made its way around the town, I made my way on foot to Tonge cemetery. I was soaked to the skin. The streets were still lined with 1000s of people. I took up position near the gates of the cemetery as the cortège came towards me. I noticed that Betsy was no longer leading the engines. I was told later that she had returned to the sheds at Radcliffe Road, after doing her duty. From where I was standing I saw all the family in the funeral cars and I could see the sadness on their faces. Fred was now only 200 yards from his final resting place.

The ground around the grave was very slippery; hundreds of mourners were gathered around the area to see Fred finally laid to rest. As the engines got nearer I noticed John Howarth (funeral director) riding on the rear of Fred's Aveling tractor as the cortège came to a final halt just 30 yards from the grave.

Fred was lowered one last time from the trailer and slowly carried to his grave. The cap that had adorned the coffin was removed and Fred was slowly lowered into his grave. Almost immediately the whistles on all the traction engines saluted one of the finest gentlemen this country has ever known. I could see tears streaming down the faces of many who were present.

One of the things that have not been made public is that after the funeral, and when the crowds had dispersed Fred's sons drove the Aveling tractor past their Dads grave, they paused for a while in reflection and then gave a final short blast on the whistle as a final goodbye gesture. The lads then took the engine back to Radcliffe Road.

I drove home again after saying goodbye to all my friends. It was a journey of reflection and sadness. I liked Fred, and his passing was a deep personal loss for me. I returned to the grave on Boxing Day. It was then while Fred's grave was covered in snow that I finally paid my respects.

Rest in peace
Paul Donoghue

113

Respected BBC film producer David Hall talks about Fred Dibnah's heritage.

Fred Dibnah – steeplejack, steam enthusiast, television presenter - Fred was many things to many people but you'd be hard pushed to find anyone who didn't admire his commitment and dedication to Britain's industrial heritage and his passion to tell everybody who cared to listen how things were built and how they worked.

Over a period of seven years from early 1998 until his untimely death in November 2004, I made more than forty programmes for the BBC with Fred. Upon his death BBC2 controller Roly Keating said "Fred Dibnah has been a much loved BBC2 face for over two decades and he is very much part of the channel's heritage." Today Fred's programmes are still as popular as ever and they are amongst the most repeated on British television. To keep this heritage alive, The View From The North was commissioned to make another twelve half hour programmes for BBC2. This commitment from the BBC along with the efforts being made by Fred's widow, Sheila, and Paul Donoghue of Rallyscene, who is releasing more of his archive, will ensure that Fred's memory and his passion for our great industrial heritage is kept alive.

Over a period of seven years from early 1998 until his untimely death in November 2004, I made more than forty programmes for the BBC with Fred

Combining footage from the programmes my company made with Fred with previously unseen material that was shot for them, this biographical series looks at the many sides of Fred - engineer, steeplejack, artist, craftsman, steam enthusiast, inventor and story teller - and at the contribution he made to our knowledge and appreciation of Britain's architectural, industrial and engineering heritage. The series looks at the way Fred helped to bring his passions for industry and engineering out of obscurity and to put them back in the public domain. When I started making the programmes with Fred in 1998, not a lot had been done on industrial history. Since then there has been a great revival of interest in this area and many experts in the field take the view that our programmes with Fred made a significant contribution to this.

Each programme in the new series features contributions from leading academics and historians, museum and industrial heritage curators, conservation groups and friends and family including Sheila Dibnah, and Fred's brother, Graham. Between them they offer a unique insight into a truly original personality who had a unique ability to explain complex subjects in a simple anecdotal way.

Fred was always great to work with and he became much more than a presenter of our programmes; he was a good friend who I would see throughout the year, not just in the summer months when we were filming. We'd hit it off from the time we first met. We both came from the same working class background in the North-West and grew up at a time when places like Bolton and Manchester, where I was from, were still the workshops of the world. I never really understood how Fred's engines worked but we shared the same passion for telling the stories of the engineers whose ingenuity and inventiveness made them possible and telling our history from the point of view of the builders and engineers and the ordinary working men who helped to make it.

We'd hit it off from the time we first met. We both came from the same working class background in the North-West

116

For seven years we spent every summer travelling the length and breadth of Britain visiting magnificent castles and cathedrals, climbing to the top of great bridges like the Forth and the Humber, searching out steam powered mill engines and pit winding engines and tunnelling beneath the earth in coal mines and long forgotten canal tunnels. I've included many of the highlights in this new series.

For Fred it was all a holiday paid for by the BBC, taking him to all these wonderful places that he wanted to go to and it was in that spirit that we made the programmes so that his enthusiasm and sense of fun was never diminished. But it wasn't without its dangers. Clambering around on the scaffolding around the dome of St Paul's or climbing up to the top of the Forth Bridge with him wasn't a problem, but wherever we went I'd always go for a pint with Fred at the end of the day and I've lost count of the number of lock ins we had as the pints were lined up on the bar for him while Fred delighted the whole bar with his stories.

This new series is, I hope, a fitting tribute to Fred and it will help to preserve his heritage and the things he stood for. Making it and writing the biography he always said he would like me to write has brought back many happy memories of my time with him. His distinctive tones still ring around our offices every day as we edit the programmes and I'm pleased that we are able to help him achieve one of his greatest wishes that he will be remembered through his programmes and live on in them to provide many more years of entertainment for his devoted fans.

Deep in thought; Jack & Fred Dibnah,
David Hall and Alf Molyneux

A Lasting Memorial to Our Fred

By
Sheila Dibnah

After my late husband's premature death, The Bolton & District Civic Trust, in conjunction with the local newspaper The Bolton Evening News, set up 'The Fred Dibnah Memorial Fund' aimed at providing a permanent memorial in his home town of Bolton, Lancashire. At the time of writing, this is expected to be in the shape of a bronze statue of Fred in the town centre, standing in a glass showcase at the side of a stationary steam engine, known as 'The Hick Hargreaves Engine'.

Although not 'officially' involved, as Fred's widow I have devoted all my spare time trying to help the appeal as much as I can. So far, I have managed to raise several thousand pounds.

I have not yet sold anything of substance, but have succeeded in placing various small items personal to Fred on the internet auction site, E-bay, which I knew his fans would like to own. The most unlikely items raised quite large amounts of money. For instance, I was pleased to see such as one of Fred's oily shirts fetching over £100, and a glass jam jar containing swarf (metal shavings) made in the workshops reached over £70. An autograph and pint glass once owned by Fred, with two empty Guinness cans chucked in attracted a bid of over £110. Two shabby used sanding discs sold for £33. People such as Simon Swift of Steam-4-fun have kindly donated valuable goods, such as two brand new model live steam engines, a Wilseco roller, and a Mamod steam wagon. Since each engine donated was the number one of a limited range of no more than 250, they brought in several hundred pounds for the fund, shortly after I put them on E-bay. Another businessman, Chris Bruce donated half the profits made from auctioning a valuable original artwork of Fred done in oils.

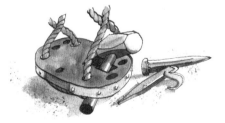

So what about the future? Well, it goes without saying there will never be anyone else like Fred again. We were very lucky to have him enrich our lives in the way he did. Thankfully, because he did so much for steam and preservation, and our industrial heritage, he brought the 'common touch' to what had previously been something of a slightly dull subject for some people. People like David Hall (A View from the North) and Paul Donoghue (Rallyscene) will continue to reach into their extensive archives, showing the world more of the man we all loved, through their films and books. During his life Fred totally endorsed these people. As Fred's widow I see no reason not to continue Fred's endorsement and help in anyway I can to keep Fred's memory alive.

To help keep the memory of Fred Dibnah alive in the form of a lasting memorial.

Please donate generously to

The Bolton & District Civic Trust
Fred Dibnah Memorial Appeal

If you would like to make a donation to The Fred Dibnah Memorial Appeal you can simply visit any branch of Lloyds TSB and mention this appeal to the cashier and make a donation.

You can also send a cheque made out to:

The Fred Dibnah Appeal
Lloyds TSB
Hotel Street
Bolton
Lancs.
BL1 1DB

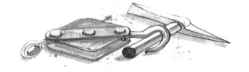

I donated my wedding bouquet to the cause. It raised £333 and even had a bright idea to auction off the pleasure of my company, along with my late husband's close friend and fellow steeplejack Eddie Chattwood. We advertised ourselves on E-bay as being willing to have a pub lunch with the winner and two friends. I am humbled to admit we only fetched 49 quid – but it was Christmas! It turned out to be great event, and the winner was Carl Hammer, a blacksmith, who subsequently went on to organise his own event to raise money for the appeal.

Another way I have succeeded in helping the fund, was to become involved in presenting 'Fred Dibnah Nights' at small theatres and village halls, with two talented friends, Alan St-John and Steve Morris, collectively known as 'Donkey Stone'. Alan and Steve use original material, songs, and monologues and amuse the audience in the second half of the show, after I have presented an audio-visual hour of my life with Fred – and some of his own amusing anecdotes! The audiences seem to love these nights, as they help keep Fred fresh in their minds. We have just started to have a raffle during the interval, and Paul Donoghue has been kind enough to donate large quantities of Rallyscenes' bone-china collectors plates and 'Fred Dibnah Remembered' DVD's to the cause, which has helped immensely and proved to be very popular indeed.

Other individuals and groups have also organised their own 'Fred nights' and this has raised a lot of money. My late husband seemed to inspire genuine loyalty in people who followed his programmes, and now they are rallying round to help this excellent cause.

Of course, for each copy of this book (sold through the Rallyscene call-centre) £1 will also be donated to the 'Fred Dibnah Memorial Fund'. May I take this opportunity to personally thank you for purchasing this publication, and helping in your own way to ensure Fred's memory lives on.

Fred Dibnah "A much loved Steeplejack"
Limited Edition A3 signed prints available. Visit www.FredDibnah.tv for purchase details

FREDS MEMORIAL STONE
"A FINAL WISH GRANTED"

BY
SHEILA DIBNAH

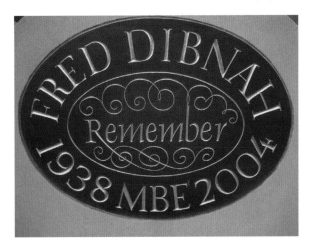

As it became obvious that Fred wasn't going to beat the cancer, we would often talk about things during our marriage that had meant a lot to us. Places we had visited, thoughts between us at the time, how we had felt. One such very special place was the Welsh Slate Museum at Llanberris in Caernarfon, Gwynnd. I had gone on location with David Hall and the film crew in 1998 during the filming of 'Industrial Age', and Fred, as ever had been struck by the sheer brutality of life as a miner in days gone by. We courted in those caverns of Welsh slate, and increasingly fell in love with each other as we wandered through the hollow bowels of the earth. Slate meant 'love' to us, and therefore we had a special word, a code we used sometimes in public to say 'I love you'. That word was 'Ivvie'. Ivvie came from a corruption of the name Ivy, because Fred made me laugh when he said to me 'Bloody cold down here, Ivy, give us a love!". Fred would often be at some event and say 'Ivvie' – only I knew what he meant!

The elliptical Welsh Slate design for instance, taken from the 'Aveling & Porter' oval plaque on 'Betsy' and engraved with the scrolled inscription *'Remember Fred Dibnah'* catches your eye as you walk past...

As I discussed Fred's headstone with Master stonemason Mark Stafford after finding his website on the internet, I told him about what I had promised Fred as he lay in hospital bed shortly before he was admitted to the Hospice. Fred told me he didn't want 'owt fancy' for his stone, nor did he want a lots of writing on it, but wanted some fancy script. He told me his life as a steeplejack was what had been most important to him, and he wished he could have lived it over again. He was a down-to-earth man, he said, and wanted something to reflect this.

I cried as I spoke with Mark and thought of Llanberris, remembering holding Fred's hand as he said 'Ivvie' all those years ago. So the design of the stone came about purely as a set of symbols which meant something special to my husband. The elliptical Welsh Slate design for instance, taken from the 'Aveling & Porter' oval

plaque on 'Betsy' and engraved with the scrolled inscription *'Remember Fred Dibnah'* catches your eye as you walk past, and pays tribute to his engineering skills. See how the letter 'b' in the word remember, forms a chimney with swirls of smoke coming out, like a traction engine or mill chimney. The gold leaf was a favourite medium of Freds. As a steeplejack, he worked many times, gilding weathervanes and clock faces. Sand stone, the main body of the memorial, was another stone he ideally liked, because of the extensive use of it in Victorian architecture, due to it being easier to work than granite or marble.

Mark and I between us came up with a fitting tribute Fred would have truly loved, a highly crafted headstone with all his values plain to see. But above all, the words *'A Much Loved Steeplejack'* means that for Fred, his final wishes will always remain. That is to be remembered as a simple soul who loved what he did.

THE WIDOW'S TALE
BY
MRS. SHEILA DIBNAH

*N*o one knows what goes on behind closed doors' laments the old Charlie Rich song.

It's true. No one really does, do they? Mind you, for reasons best known to themselves, there are many negative people out there willing to speculate on my marriage to my late husband. When like me, you don't court publicity on private matters. Rumours run rife, tales are told, and some amplified beyond all recognition – and all seemingly dismissing one significant thing, that Fred and I were husband and wife... and what happens between husband and wife is usually – apart from immediate family – a very private matter. Behind closed doors, just like the song.

When we met, I found my soul mate, someone who I could love and trust for a very long time. Fred was 100% genuine.

I married Fred fully knowing that he was public property, and that as far as my man was concerned wearing his heart on his sleeve came naturally. He spoke of everything within his heart to those who would listen. It was a certain naivety; a lovely, open, lolloping honesty that could take you by surprise. This highly sensitive man was assured enough of his own masculinity to cry at times, yet strong enough to carry the burden within his heart of two failed marriages and yet; decided to give matrimony another go with me in 1998. And I loved him too, oh yes indeed – I really did love Fred, and still do. To me, he is a hero, a one-off – my 'Hippo' the pet nickname he responded to behind those same closed doors when we held each other tight. The twenty years age gap between us made no difference whatsoever, because we were in love, and love is unconditional and knows no boundaries.

Fred was little bit chauvinistic, but that was his Victorian sensibilities coming through, part of the things that shaped his world, who he was, what he did. He would expect his tea on the table at a certain time, etc. but none of that really mattered, it was a small price to pay for knowing I had a cast-iron relationship; he certainly would never cheat on me, that's for sure. He often told me he loved me... and meant it too.

Fred was a one-woman man, despite having the occasional attentions of women thrust upon him. I remember with amusement a deranged lady (nicknamed by Fred) 'Miss Two-Parrots' (his unlikely stalker) who would ring up demanding to speak with him. The situation came about through a fan letter, which Fred had answered in an over-friendly tone. The woman managed to find our telephone number, and decided Fred was going to be her man? We laughed off things like this, and were mostly happy until illness struck, and then it all radically changed...

Unless you have lived through the sheer torture of watching a person you love die from a terminal disease, it leaves you feeling helpless and unable to change the cause, or effects, you will not be able to comprehend what hell is like. Initially with Fred it was a very private hell - despite the relentless, constant influx of well-meaning people surrounding him in what were to be his final months. During this period this sometimes made me feel worthless, and on occasions, unable to stay emotionally close to my husband. His mind was being gradually taken over by the effects of morphine, and on frequent occasions, other people's wishes became mixed up with his own, and this meant things between Fred and I became uncomfortable. "What are we doing falling out cock, we shouldn't be arguing at a time like this, he used to say?" The doctors had ordered complete rest, but Fred was like a man on a mission, and ignored the best of advice.

How many men do you know who would be physically able to climb up a ladder and undertake the heavy task of creosoting after two gruelling cycles of chemotherapy, and increasingly failing health? One Sunday, I came home after spending a few hours with my mum, to find Fred laid up in bed after having fallen twelve feet off his pithead gear in the back yard. I learned from others who were present that he'd insisted on doing the job himself, despite many offers of help. This was so typical of him. He had hurt his back, caused a massive bruise, and covered himself from head to foot in stinking creosote. Yet to him it was simply a case of 'naaa...it's 'nowt, cock'. He had hurt himself all right, and this happened when he was in the middle of filming his last television series 'Made in Britain' with David Hall. Fred was due to go off on location the very next morning at 8am. Looking at him in bed, and seeing him in such pain, I was sure he would not make it – but, make it he did. Next morning he was up early, scrubbed, dressed, breakfasted, ready and waiting for the car to arrive, rubbing his back and feeling poorly from the accident, but still he made it to work. What a man!

As the illness took its toll, I watched his energy fail and the bright aura of his effervescent personality fade into nothingness where instead, ultimately lay a small, pale waif-like figure in a hospital bed, vulnerable and overwhelmed by the implications of his terrible illness with a name that strikes dread into your inner soul.

My feelings remain the same for Fred as they have always done, I will never marry again and I know time is a great healer , but in my eyes, no one else could ever live up to the mark. I had the very best – and worst - of Fred that is for certain, because we understood each other (at least until he became ill), and as a result, I am left with a myriad of happy, treasured memories. People who knew him well, real friends such as David Hall, Alan McEwen, Alf Molyneux, Jimmy Crooks, Peter Lidgett, Ian Thompson, Eddie Chattwood, Michael Webber, Derek Roscoe – to name but a few, have all stood by and supported me through the awful ordeal of losing my famous husband. They know the background of what I had to cope with, what happened to Fred. Adversaries and moral judges do not matter to me; Fred was my man and a great husband.

Fred was tough, nothing was going to stop his determination to accomplish as much as possible before he became too ill. I felt that I was in his way, so I faded into the background and let Fred and his men get on with the job in hand. All my fussing and fretting was getting me nowhere. So rightly or wrongly I allowed Fred's men to take pole position. Fred's Aveling and Porter engine had to be completed at all costs.

Apart from help from my son Nathan, I nursed Fred single-handedly through his illness. It was only when he became bed-ridden, did I receive any help from the medical profession, but mostly I coped alone until a time came near the end when I couldn't get near the bed for other people in the room, friends, estranged family, cronies, strangers, hangers-on, all unwilling to leave, taking my place forever in his life. It got to the point where I would visit Fred early in the morning or last thing at night. The last thing he ever said to me "Thanks for looking after me, cock". I will never forget that as long as I live, the memory of those words will stay with me forever. But we married for better or for worse, in sickness and in health I could not and would not desert Fred now.

When Paul Donoghue first approached me about taking part in this book, I was very sceptical indeed and wanted no part in it.

127

When Paul Dongohue first approached me about taking part in this book, I was very sceptical indeed and wanted no part in it. I considered him an outsider, because in the past, there had been some bad feeling between us over his film footage taken at Fred's funeral. Some of you may have read about this in 'Old Glory' when I sounded off about Paul filming in the cemetery, and the resulting DVD, which I disparagingly referred to as his 'get-dead-with-Fred' video. Yet, when I took time to watch the film, I was moved to tears by the sensitive way in which Paul had offered the nation the lasting tribute to his good friend Fred Dibnah, and I recalled the warmth in my husband's voice when he often spoke about Paul in the past. That is why I agreed to be included in this book; it is what Fred would have wanted.

Paul holds high regard for Fred and all that he achieved and, through their lengthy time spent together as friends and business associates, you are able to see a side of Fred not yet made public, Fred gave Paul mountains of material with a view to writing a candid, in-depth book many years ago. It is very sad it never came to fruition, but Paul felt that the time was not right, due to Fred being upset and bitter about the demise of his second marriage.

Of course, there are many interviews out there with people claiming to know Fred extremely well, and just as many casual acquaintances jumping on the bandwagon claiming to have a close friendship with him. All this needs putting firmly into perspective. If you met Fred and talked to him – he would treat you as if he had known you all his life. It was one of his gifts to make people feel special. If you met him twenty years ago – you then meet again years later, suddenly, bingo! You are close mates, with all the kudos that entails.

There were times Fred infuriated me, for instance, when we were out trying to have a quiet drink, and a stranger would come over "Hello Fred, you don't know me..." By the time they left, sometimes hours later, they felt a connection with this special man that would quite often change their lives. This is no exaggeration; I have been overwhelmed with kindness from the public since Fred died. Yet, by contrast, there were very few 'real friends' in Fred's life, because essentially, he was a loner, his mind was always on the next project in the garden, or some chimney felling job to do, but he would always make time for a chat. He loved people.

Both Paul Donoghue and David Hall with their work have successfully preserved for you the very essence of Fred. I support them both in their quest, and am pleased to see their determination in making sure the nation will never forget 'Our Fred'. Through my own extensive diaries, personal recordings, and photographs, it is my dearest wish to publish my own book (when the time is right), outlining my time with the clever, funny, unique and highly skilled articulate working-class man who became the expert on steam and industrial history – and the love of my life.

People sometimes say to me "What did you learn from your marriage to Fred?" I tell them. Do not be afraid of being yourself no matter what others think. Everyone is equal, no matter what your background. Most importantly, people and hard work matter most.

Without Fred, this world is a much sadder place, and those of us who truly loved him will never let you forget that special place he holds in your heart too. This book is for you and me.

Sheila Dibnah

Opus64

Layout designer of this book

Fred Dibnah A much Loved Steeplejack

dvd	**create**
video	**cd-rom**

Working with Rallyscene

Editor of the acclaimed DVD Video
"Remembering Fred Dibnah"

Designer of the Rallyscene website

VIDEO PRODUCTION ■ GRAPHICS ■ MULTIMEDIA ■ DVD VIDEO

T: 0115 9461819   E: David@opus64.co.uk   www.opus64.co.uk

Brian Smith is a Sheffield-based artist with expertise in
a wide range of art forms; from Fine Art, including
portraiture, landscape and the built environment; to
murals, cartoons and caricatures, all to the highest
professional standards. Although primarily a
water-colourist, subjects can also be rendered as
superb quality black and white drawings. Brian's
innovative line and wash illustrations feature
throughout the book "Fred Dibnah a well loved
Steeplejack", and his work has been used in calendar,
corporate greetings card and even jigsaw designs.
Commissioned paintings are in private collections
around the world. His portfolio encompasses
architectural illustrations such as a portrait of your
home or corporate headquarters, as well as the
preparation of perspective illustrations for architects
and developers from working drawings and site
photographs. An ongoing commitment to running
painting courses, workshops and demonstrations is
complemented by a wide experience in preparing and
delivering Art and Design programmes through
residences in schools from Y4 level upwards, to
dovetail with and enhance the national curriculum.

Clients include;
Royal Collection Enterprises
The BBC
Alzheimer's Society
Rotherham Borough Council

A full range of work and services can be viewed at
www.BrianSmithArtist.co.uk
A professional service, on time and in budget is guaranteed.

To discuss your particular requirements contact
Brian@fineartist.wanadoo.co.uk
104 Little Norton Lane, Sheffield S8 8GD Tel: 0114 2747339 or 0771 4262139

WANT SOMETHING DIFFERENT FOR YOUR EVENT?

Using all her showgirl experience, Sheila has crafted a remarkable entertaining show
about her life with, and the life and times of her famous husband Fred Dibnah.
"This truly is 'THE OTHER HALF OF FRED' - don't miss this exciting opportunity to
lift the cap on this celebrated steeplejack and family man.
No one else can give you the real 'nuts and bolts' of Fred Dibnah.
Hear the stories, laugh at his antics.
Be amazed at the candour and wicked impersonations!
Sheila is available nationwide for After Dinner Talks, theatre shows,
personal appearance work, photo shoots, cruise line bookings.
Contact www.Dibnahs.com Telephone 01246 811112
for all available dates and further details